"'So many books,' a phrase usually muttered with despair, is transformed into an expression of awe and joy by Gabriel Zaid. Arguing that books are *the* essential part of the great conversation we call culture and civilization, *So Many Books* reminds us that reading (and, by extension, writing and publishing) is a business, a vanity, a vocation, an avocation, a moral and political act, a hedonistic pursuit, all of the aforementioned, none of the aforementioned, and is often a miracle."
— Doug Dutton, Owner of Dutton's Brentwood Books

"Gabriel Zaid is a marvelously elegant and playful writer—a cosmopolitan critic with sound judgment and a light touch. He is a jewel of Latin American letters, which is no small thing to be. Read him—you'll see."
— Paul Berman, Author of *Terror and Liberalism*

"Gabriel Zaid's defense of books is genuinely exhilarating. It is not pious, it is wise; and its wisdom is delivered with extraordinary lucidity and charm. This is how Montaigne would have written about the dizzy and increasingly dolorous age of the Internet. May *So Many Books* fall into so many hands."
— Leon Wieseltier, Literary Editor of the *New Republic*

"Gabriel Zaid's small gem of a book manages to be both delectable and useful, like chocolate fortified with vitamins. His rare blend of wisdom and savvy practical sense should make essential and heartening reading for anyone who cares about the future of books and the life of the mind."
— Lynne Sharon Schwartz, Author of *Ruined by Reading: A Life in Books*

"A truly original book about books. Destined to be a classic."
— Enrique Krauze, Author of *Mexico: Biography of Power*,
Editor of *Letras Libres*

"With cascades of books pouring down on him from every direction, how can the twenty-first-century reader keep his head above water? Gabriel Zaid answers that question in a variety of surprising ways, many of th━━ ━ ━ ━, all of them provocative."
— A━━ F━━━━━ ━━━━ ━ ━━ ━━━ *ican Scholar*, Author of *Ex Libris*

PAUL DRY BOOKS

Philadelphia   2003

SO MANY BOOKS

Reading and Publishing
in an Age of Abundance

by GABRIEL ZAID

Translated by Natasha Wimmer

First Paul Dry Books Edition, 2003

Paul Dry Books, Inc.
Philadelphia, Pennsylvania
www.pauldrybooks.com

Text type: Cochin
Display type: Zapf Renaissance Book
Composed by P. M. Gordon Associates, Inc.
Designed by Adrianne Onderdonk Dudden

1 3 5 7 9 8 6 4 2
Printed in the United States of America

Library of Congress Cataloging-in-Publication Data
Zaid, Gabriel.
  [Los demasiados libros. English]
  So many books : reading and publishing in an age of abundance /
by Gabriel Zaid ; translated by Natasha Wimmer. — 1st Paul Dry
Books ed.
     p.   cm.
  ISBN 1-58988-003-X (alk. paper)
  1. Books and reading. 2. Book industries and trade. 3. Publishers
and publishing. I. Title.
Z1003.Z1513 2003
028'.9—dc21

                                              2003007643

On the cover: Argument #5, 8,000 books (1999)
By Tom Bendtsen. Photograph by the artist.

Contents

SO MANY BOOKS

To the Unrepentant Reader

THE READING OF BOOKS is growing arithmetically; the writing of books is growing exponentially. If our passion for writing goes unchecked, in the near future there will be more people writing books than reading them.

Midway through the fifteenth century, when books were first printed, a few hundred titles were published each year, in editions of hundreds of copies. Most were ancient texts (Biblical, Greek, Roman, or the works of the church fathers) or explications and commentaries on those same texts, although some contemporary works were allowed to mingle with the classics. Perhaps this is why we have felt ever since that to see our words in type is to be consecrated, to be immortalized.

At the beginning of the twenty-first century, our universal graphomania produces a million titles a year, in printings of thousands of copies. Very few books are reprinted; even fewer are translated. Many authors don't write for their readers, but to pad their resumés. At the other extreme are those who write for the market, and make money by educating, informing, or entertaining. The books we cherish are the exceptions: old books worthy of rereading (the classics) and contemporary books written in the same tradition.

This tradition is a robust one, which has been enriched by the innovations that seemed to threaten it. When the book first appeared, Socrates rejected it as inferior to conversation. When the printing press first appeared, some stubborn readers refused to permit industrial products in their libraries and hired scribes to copy printed books. When the television first appeared, the end of the book was proclaimed. The same happened with the arrival of the CD-ROM and the e-book. When the market began to consolidate around a few bestsellers, chain stores, online booksellers, and publishing conglomerates, it was feared that diversity would suffer. But huge sales for a few titles don't mean that all other books will disappear—rather, that those other books are relatively obscure. Our new technologies (the Internet, print-on-demand) are increasing the millions of titles available. And the conversation continues, unheeded by television, which will never report: "Yesterday, a student read Socrates' *Apology* and felt free."

The freedom and happiness experienced in reading are addictive, and the strength of the tradition lies in that experience, which ultimately turns all innovations to its own ends. Reading liberates the reader and transports him from his book to a reading of himself and all of life. It leads him to participate in conversations, and in some cases to arrange them, as so many active readers do: parents, teachers, friends, writers, translators, critics, publishers, booksellers, librarians, promoters.

The uniqueness of each reader, reflected in the particular nature of his personal library (his intellectual genome), flourishes in diversity. And the conversation continues, between the excesses of graphomania and the excesses of commerce, between the sprawl of chaos and the concentration of the market.

An Embarrassment of Books

THOSE WHO ASPIRE to the status of cultured individuals visit bookstores with trepidation, overwhelmed by the immensity of all they have not read. They buy something that they've been told is good, make an unsuccessful attempt to read it, and when they have accumulated half a dozen unread books, feel so bad that they are afraid to buy more.

In contrast, the truly cultured are capable of owning thousands of unread books without losing their composure or their desire for more.

"Every private library is a reading plan," Spanish philosopher José Gaos once wrote. So accurate is this observation that in order for it also to be ironic the reader must acknowledge a kind of general unspoken assumption: a book not read is a project uncompleted. Having unread books on display is like writing checks when you have no money in the bank—a way of deceiving your guests.

Ernest Dichter, in his *Handbook of Consumer Motivations*, speaks of this guilty conscience as it affects mail-order book club members. There are those who sign up with the idea that they are gaining entrance to a cultural extravaganza. But as the books arrive and the time required to read them adds up, each new shipment becomes a less-than-festive reproach, an accusation of failure. Finally the discouraged members withdraw, resentful that books are still being sent, even though they have paid for them.

This explains the invention of books that aren't meant to be read. Books, in other words, that can be displayed without consequences or guilt: dictionaries, encyclopedias, atlases, art books, cookbooks, reference books, bibliographies, anthologies, complete works. Books that tasteful gift-givers prefer—because they're expensive, which is a sign of esteem, and because they don't threaten the recipient with the task of responding to the questions "Have you read it yet? What did you think of it?" In fact, the most uncommercial slogan in the world might be: "Give a book! It's like giving an obligation."

Authors aren't so mindful of their readers. Even excepting the extreme cases (those writers who call to see what page you're on, when you'll finish, and above all, when you'll publish a long, intelligent, and objective review), they feel obliged to bestow obligations each time they publish. It is understood that the elegant sidestep in such cases is to reply immediately with a card that reads: "I just received your book. What a wonderful surprise! I congratulate you, and I congratulate myself in advance for the pleasure that reading it will give me." (Mexican writer Alfonso Reyes used printed cards, with blank spaces for the date, name, and title.) Otherwise, the debt multiplies and compounds as time passes, until the moment comes when the pending responsibility of reading the book, writing a letter (which can no longer be so short), and coming up with praise that isn't false or faint becomes a nightmare. It's hard to say whether this or the card sent by return mail is worse.

But there is more: what to do, physically, with the book? The author might appear one day and discover it in pristine, untouched condition. A good strategy, which unfortunately also requires discipline, is to ruffle the first pages upon receiving it and insert a bookmark as proof of your good intentions. Or make it disappear, explaining (if necessary) that a friend was so excited to see it that she borrowed it before you could read it. In this case, it is prudent to remove the dedication page: signed books have an unfortunate habit of ending up in the hands of dealers, and there are terrible stories about books by Rilke fulsomely dedicated to Valéry and later found in bookstalls on the Seine. Or there is the story about the Mexican author who found his book —uncut —in a used bookstore, and bought and resent it to his friend, "With the renewed affection of Artemio de Valle-Arizpe."

A terrible solution is to keep books until you've accumulated a library of thousands of volumes, all the while telling yourself that you know you don't have the time to read them but that you'll be able to leave them to your children. This is an excuse that grows weaker and weaker as science makes ever greater strides. Almost all books are obsolete from the moment they're written, if not before. And marketing strategies engineer the planned obsolescence even of classic authors (with new and better critical editions) to eliminate the ruinous transmission of tastes from one generation to the next, which once upon a time so stifled the market.

The creation of an obsolete library for one's children may only be justified in the way that the preservation of ruins is justified: in the name of archaeology. Better excuses exist for collecting books than the construction of a library for posterity. If you amass a collection dedicated to the history of the Mexican state of Tlaxcala, or, better yet, of editions of *Don Quixote*, no one can expect you to have read *Don Quixote* thousands of times, once for each edition—though plenty of innocent visitors will be scandalized to see the same title repeated over and over. Isn't it a little like having your picture taken thousands of times and from thousands of angles with the only big fish you ever caught in your life?

In keeping with the Categorical Imperative of Reading and Being Cultured, a library is a trophy room. *The Magic Mountain* is like an elephant's foot, lending prestige, serving as a footstool, and prompting the discussion of dangerous trips to Africa. And what about the lion who winked an eye at the hunter before falling at his feet? Thus, the owner of Churchill's memoirs, signed and unread, can say: "Poor Winston! I'm keeping them as they were when I got them, out of respect for his memory. What a formidable British lion! I begged the taxidermist to be careful to preserve the wink . . ."

Hunters are famous for exaggerating. That is why it is a matter of professional ethics for the reader who aspires to be cultured never to display pieces that haven't been properly bagged—not to mention pieces that were actually read by a friend, or the guide, on cultural safari. As a result, a book can only be seen as a dissected cadaver, not a captive live animal. Tigers in the gas tank? All right. But roaring all over the house, lounging in the bathroom or on the bed, stretching and yawning in the windows, perched on shelves? Never! Out of respect for one's guests.

The Categorical Imperative derives from the old belief in the sacredness of books. In *In Search of a Better World*, Karl Popper surmises that Western democratic culture was born with the establishment of the book market in Athens, in the fifth century before Christ: the book as commercial product did away with the book as sacred object. But did it really? The market is ambivalent. To have at home and at hand what once could only be viewed in the temple is a great boon for demand, because books embody all the prestige of the temple. Democratic desacralization flourishes like simony: it allows the selling of something priceless. It doesn't do away with sacred books; it causes them to multiply.

Socrates criticized the fetishization of the book (*Phaedrus*). Two centuries later in another book-centered culture (the Biblical world), it was written in Ecclesiastes (12:12) that ". . . of making many books there is no end; and much study is a weariness of the flesh." In the first century, Seneca wrote to Lucilius "In the multitude of books is distraction." Ibn Khaldun, in the fourteenth century: "Too many books on a subject make it more difficult to study" (*The Muqaddimah*, VI, 27). Montaigne: "To compose our character is our duty, not to compose books" (*Essays*, III, 13). Don Quixote, upon learning of the writing of *Don Quixote:* "There are those who compose books and pop them out like so many buns" (II, 3). Samuel Johnson: "No place affords a more striking conviction of the vanity of human hopes than a public library; for who can see the wall crowded on every side by mighty volumes, the works of laborious meditations and accurate inquiry, now scarcely known but by the catalogue . . ." (*Rambler* No. 106, March 23, 1751).

I once proposed a chastity glove for authors who were unable to contain themselves. But an icy plunge works too: like Johnson, writers can try submersion in a great library, among a multitude of neglected authors, to discourage themselves. Progress has ordered things so that all citizens, not just the prophets, may give themselves the luxury of preaching in the desert.

What could bring a halt to the proliferation of books? For a time, it seemed as if television might. Marshall McLuhan wrote (wrote!) prophetic books about the end of the age of the book. But the explosion of publishing left McLuhan himself preaching in the desert.

Until 1947, there were only seven commercial television channels in the United States, which became 50 in 1949 (when the major networks appeared) and 517 in 1960. From 1947 to 1960, the percentage of households with television sets jumped from almost zero to 88 percent. The stage was thus set for the demise of the book. Nevertheless, the number of titles published each year in the same period more than doubled: from seven thousand to fifteen thousand. Even more surprising, from 1960 to 1968, the number of titles doubled again, and in a shorter period, whereas the number of homes with television sets could naturally only rise to the saturation point: 98 percent (*Statistical Abstract of the United States*).

In the middle of the fifteenth century, the printing press with movable type appeared in Europe. It didn't immediately replace the copyists, or printing with wooden blocks, but it made many more titles available. From 1450 to 1500, between 10,000 and 15,000 titles were published (the so-called incunabula) in 30,000 to 35,000 editions, with average printings of 500 copies, according to Lucien Febvre and Henri-Jean Martin (*The Coming of the Book: The Impact of Printing 1450–1800*) — say 250 titles per year, starting with 100 in 1450. By 1952, 250,000 were being published (Robert Escarpit, *The Book Revolution*). This implies a rate of growth five times that of the population.

It was assumed that television would put an end to both explosions, but that end never came, as can be seen in the statistics for the year 2000, extrapolated from the *Unesco Statistical Yearbook 1999.*

Since the invention of the television, the world population has grown 1.8 percent each year (as compared to 0.3 percent annually over the preceding five hundred years) and the publication of books has grown 2.8 percent (as compared to 1.6 percent).

Date	1450 (Gutenberg)	1950 (Television)	2000
Titles per year	100	250,000	1,000,000
Population (in millions)	500	2,500	6,000
Titles per million inhabitants	0.2	100	167

From these rough figures, some rough interpolations may be made. Five hundred titles were published in 1550, 2,300 in 1650, 11,000 in 1750, and 50,000 in 1850. In 1550, the cumulative bibliography was approximately 35,000 titles; in 1650 it was 150,000; in 1750 it was 700,000; in 1850 it was 3.3 million; in 1950 it was 16 million; and in 2000 it was 52 million. In the first century of printing (1450–1550), 35,000 titles were published; in the last half-century (1950–2000), there were a thousand times more, 36 million.

The human race publishes a book every thirty seconds. Supposing an average price of thirty dol-

lars per book and an average thickness of two centimeters, thirty million dollars and close to fifteen
miles of shelves would be required for the yearly
addition to Mallarmé's library, if today the poet
wished to be able to say:

The flesh is sad, alas! and I've read all the books.

Books are published at such a rapid rate that
they make us exponentially more ignorant. If a
person read a book a day, he would be neglecting
to read four thousand others, published the same
day. In other words, the books he didn't read
would pile up four thousand times faster than the
books he did read, and his ignorance would grow
four thousand times faster than his knowledge.

"There is so much to learn and so little time to
live," as Baltasar Gracián wrote. But once again,
the aphorism functions poetically, transcending its
quantitative truth, its melancholic tone erasing the
feelings of guilt aroused by our finiteness in the
face of the infinite tasks demanded by the Categorical Imperative. Yes, there is something deeply
sad about visiting a library or bookstore full of

books that we will never read. Something that brings to mind the following lines by Borges:

> There is a mirror that has seen me for the last time.
> There is a door I have shut until the end of the
> world.
> Among the books in my library (I have them before
> me)
> There are some I shall never reopen.

Why read? And why write? After reading one hundred, one thousand, ten thousand books in a lifetime, what have we read? Nothing. To say "I only know that I've read nothing," after reading thousands of books, is not false modesty. It is strictly accurate, to the first decimal place of zero percent. But is that not perhaps exactly, Socratically, what our embarrassment of books should teach us? To be aware of our ignorance, to fully accept it; to go from being simply ignorant to being consciously ignorant?

Maybe our understanding of our finiteness is the only access we have to the totality that beckons and vanquishes us, that creates an outsize totalizing ambition in us. Maybe all experience of infinity is an illusion, if it is not precisely an experience of finiteness. And maybe the measure of our reading should therefore be, not the number of books we've read, but the state in which they leave us.

What does it matter how cultivated and up-to-date we are, or how many thousands of books we've read? What matters is how we feel, how we see, what we do after reading; whether the street and the clouds and the existence of others mean anything to us; whether reading makes us, physically, more alive.

Complaining About Babel

ALMOST ALL BOOKS sell thousands of copies, not dozens or hundreds of thousands, let alone millions. It is said—unthinkingly—that this is a bad thing.

A film requires hundreds of thousands of viewers to justify the investment. What is the fate of films that could never attract such large audiences? They aren't made. As a result, the number of films produced worldwide is not even 1 percent of the number of books published. If books were to cost as much as films to produce and distribute (as some do, like encyclopedias), an audience of hundreds of thousands would be required—a Hollywood-size audience. And what would happen to the 99 percent of books that could never sell hundreds of thousands of copies? No one would publish them.

Books are so cheap that, unlike newspapers, radio, or television, they can be published advertisement-free for a few thousand interested readers. To finance almost any book, it is enough to find three thousand readers willing to pay six hours worth of minimum-wage salary. Naturally, if thirty thousand readers could be reached, it would be possible to lower the price—by half, say. But it isn't easy to reach thirty thousand readers. Not because the lower price is still too high, but for a reason we prefer to ignore: the majority of titles published are of no interest to thirty thousand people—you couldn't even give away that many copies.

Book people (authors and readers, publishers and booksellers, librarians and teachers) have a habit of feeling sorry for themselves, a tendency to complain even when all is well. This makes them see as a failure something that is actually a blessing: The book business, unlike newspapers, films, or television, is viable on a small scale. In the case of books, the economic threshold, or the minimum investment required to gain access to the market, is very low, which encourages the proliferation of titles and publishing houses, the flourishing of various and disparate initiatives, and an abundance of cultural richness. If the threshold of viability were as high as it is for the mass media, there would be less diversity, as is true of mass media. Let us suppose that only one of every hundred titles were published, but for readerships the size of film audiences. What advantage would that scenario offer? None at all, because those titles are already being published today: they're our bestsellers. On the other hand, the ninety-nine books not of interest to a huge public would be lost. The film business requires the elimination of perhaps as many as 99 percent of all possible films. The book business doesn't. If the book is appropriate for a broader public, it can reach a broader public. If it isn't, it may still be viable, as long as it is of interest to a few thousand readers.

What reasons are there for demanding that all books sell millions of copies? Vanity (the author's, the publisher's) or national pride? If a book, as compared to a film, is commercially viable even if it doesn't interest more than a few people, why not publish it? It is natural that a more populous, richer, better-educated society should fuel demand for certain titles, but it doesn't follow that such a society should therefore stop publishing books that sell fewer copies. On the contrary, as the population of a country increases and it becomes richer and better educated, it paradoxically publishes more titles with lower sales: the variety of specialties and interests grows, and it becomes easier to attract a few thousand readers interested in something very specific. The number of titles that are viable in printings of a few thousand copies rises.

This situation allows us to understand a little-known fact, one of those facts that is hardly ever stated, since it defies conventional wisdom: Most of the titles published in rich countries sell no more than a few thousand copies, just as is true in the rest of the world. How can this be? Isn't there always talk about massive printings? There is talk, and these printings do exist, but they exist side by side with small printings, which are the majority and are never discussed. The true editorial superiority of rich countries lies in their ability to more easily reach a few thousand buyers willing to pay thirty dollars (or much more) for a book of very limited appeal. It lies in the fact that they publish ten times more titles per capita than poorer countries, because they are able to afford the luxury of publishing an infinite variety of titles in small printings.

In many areas, progress destroys diversity. Not so with books. After Gutenberg, mass market journalism, film, television, computing, satellite communications, and the Internet have all appeared. With each new development, the end of the book was prophesied, and each time more books were published, with greater ease and on more diverse subjects. Now, print-on-demand systems make printings of fifty or one hundred copies cost-effective. And what does this mean? It has become possible to publish books that interest no more than fifty or one hundred people. Of course, there will always be some author who, instead of appreciating the benefits of this system, will say, "How is it possible that no more than fifty (or one hundred) copies of my *Deconstructive Hermeneutics* have been sold! There must be a conspiracy against me. Publishers and booksellers are in it for the money—they only promote books that are easy to sell. How will humanity, numbed by television and consumerism, hermeneutically deconstruct itself? Nothing will change until Everything changes . . ."

But let us suppose that, at last, Everything does change; that the Golden Age is upon us; that a universal library system is established (a great Library of Babel) that holds every book ever published, more than fifty million titles; that every human being is allowed to collect a salary for dedicating himself solely to the reading of books; that, under these conditions, each reader is able to read four books a week, two hundred a year, ten thousand in a half-century. It would be as nothing. If not a single book were published from this moment on, it would still take 250,000 years for us to acquaint ourselves with those books already written. Simply reading a list of them (author and title) would take some fifteen years. When we say that books should be read by everyone, we aren't thinking. Our simple physical limitations make it impossible for us to read 99.9 percent of the books that are written.

Humankind writes more than it can read. If for every book published one or two languish unpublished, then two or three million books are written each year. Xlibris, "a strategic partner of Random House Ventures" specializing in vanity publishing, estimates that for every book published in the

United States there are nine unpublished manuscripts (*Harper's Magazine*, December 2000). And yet a full-time reader can't read more than two hundred, one out of every ten or fifteen thousand.

Would it be desirable for just a few books to be published each year, books that everyone in the world could read? Each of us dreams of having the world's full attention, of everyone else falling silent to hear what we have to say, of everyone else giving up writing in order to read what we have written. There exists a belief that at least a few things should be read by the whole world. But what could be said to everyone? If there were a permanent universal assembly, at which a microphone was passed around so that each person could speak to the crowd, we would scarcely have time to say hello and sit down. The universal dialogue would be reduced to a recognition of the self, a kind of Babelian poem of creation consisting of everyone saying "Good morning" to one another. Maybe that is what life is: We stand up and say hello and then disappear. But it is difficult to accept that idea. In our hello is a yearning for eternity, a yearning that makes us cling fiercely to the microphone and leads to totalitarian communion. Everyone must listen to what I have to say. The never-ending salutation is the expression of a never-ending *I*, echoing from the center of the universe. It resounds in the speeches of the Führer; in Mao's *Little Red Book*; in Psalm 49:

> Hear this, all ye people; give ear, all ye inhabitants
>   of the world:
> Both low and high, rich and poor, together.
> My mouth shall speak of wisdom; and the medita-
>   tion of my heart shall be of understanding.

It is a noble temptation, that desire to seize the microphone, to refuse to let the world go (for its own good), to subject it to one's wise words and good intentions. Nevertheless, even at gatherings of specialists the conversation must be broken up when the crowd reaches a certain size, so that the participants don't dwell on generalities and are able to address more subjects, able to say more, in smaller groups. There is no such thing as an infinite capacity for communication. Even supposing that every specialist had the same expertise and interest in every subject, there would be no time to address all subjects in a general gathering. Our simple physical limitations decree that as the number of participants rises, the average time for dialogue decreases. The participation of the whole world in a conversation doesn't enrich the dialogue; it diminishes it.

Imagine an agora, a marketplace, a cocktail party, where multiple conversations are underway. The microphone appears. The many circles become one circle, different conversations become the same conversation. Is this a good thing?

It is a myth: a myth of transparency, of the Tower of Babel replaced by a totalitarian *I*. We complain about the confusion of languages, the multiplicity of conversations, because we dream of the world's undivided attention, beyond the grasp of our finiteness. But culture is a conversation without a center. The true universal culture isn't the utopian Global Village, gathered around a microphone; it is the Babel-like multitude of villages, each the center of the world. The universality accessible to us is the finite, limited, concrete universality of diverse and disparate conversations.

Books and Conversation

THANKS TO BOOKS, we know that Socrates distrusted books. He compared them to conversation and believed they fell short. He told Phaedrus that writing is a simulation of speech, which may seem an aid to memory, knowledge, and imagination, but is ultimately counterproductive. People rely on it and fail to develop their memory, knowledge, or imagination. Even worse, they begin to believe they know things because they own books.

Conversation depends on those who take part in it: who they are, what they know, what interests them, what they've just said. In contrast, books are unfeeling monologues: They ignore the circumstances in which they're read. They repeat the same things over and over, without taking the reader into account. They pay no heed to his questions or responses.

An author's ideas suffer the same fate, being exposed to incomprehension and separated from their creator, who is not present to explain or defend them.

Books represent the harvest, not the creative process. On the other hand, ideas sown in conversation sprout and produce new ideas.

In sum, intelligence, experience, and the creative life develop and are propagated through live speech, not dead letters.

This argument embodies a criticism of progress that dates back to prehistoric times. It is the resistance to fire in the hearth and domesticated plants in the garden; the battle of the natural versus the artificial, the raw versus the cooked, the live versus the dead. Paradoxically, these arguments reach us via the medium they reject. Socrates, true to his convictions, didn't record them. Maybe Phaedrus committed them to memory—Socratically—and repeated them in other conversations, with Plato eagerly listening. Maybe Plato himself, realizing the incongruity of copying down what he had heard, had a moment of doubt. Fortunately for us, he opted to write: he was Socratic and anti-Socratic at the same time. He brought to life in books the dialogues that still question our bookish lives today.

The same questions are raised, thousands of years later, about the printed word, film, music, television, computers. For example, musicians chide us for listening to background music while we busy ourselves at other tasks. The truly musical thing, the Socratic thing, would be to meet with friends to play, to improvise a jazz dialogue dependent on the players, the mood, the inspiration . . .

But who can complain, two hundred years after Mozart's death, about being offered a compact disc collection of all his compositions? Who can complain about possessing the complete works of Plato? Today it is easy to buy such treasures, at prices that seem excessive but are actually negligible. Just compare them to the cost of buying a cathedral or a single painting by Van Gogh. Or to the cost of sitting down and carefully reading all of Plato's dialogues, or listening to all of Mozart's music.

Today it is easier to acquire treasures than it is to give them the time they deserve. And so the arguments of Socrates weigh on us, waiting on the bookshelf for our notice, and Mozart's themes come and go with little fanfare, like the sound of the wind in the trees, which fades and is lost or suddenly asserts itself and transports us.

Modern productivity reduces the cost of mechanical reproduction and increases the cost of Socratic reproduction. Intelligent conversations like those engaged in by Socrates and Phaedrus, who meet on the street, begin discussing a clever passage by Lycias on love, and go for a walk outside of Athens to debate its meaning, are only possible in an underdeveloped world, where productivity is low and there is plenty of free time. In the modern world, with everyone traveling by car, and leaving just enough time to get where they are going, Socrates and Phaedrus would never meet. And in the unlikely event that they did, it would be hard for them to find a place to stop, not to mention the time. It is hardly to be expected that they would cancel their plans like two idlers just to talk.

Confronted with the choice between having time and having things, we've chosen to have things. Today it is a luxury to read what Socrates said, not because the books are expensive, but because our time is scarce. Today intelligent conversation and contemplative leisure cost infinitely

more than the accumulation of cultural treasures.
We now have more books than we can possibly
read. The knowledge accumulated in our print
culture infinitely surpasses the learning of Socrates. In a survey of reading habits today, Socrates
would score low. His scant scholarship and his
lack of academic titles, foreign languages, resumé,
and published work would prevent him from com-
peting for important posts in the cultural bureau-
cracy, which would confirm his criticism of the
written word: The simulation and credentials of
learning have come to carry more weight than
learning itself.

But the written word, that dry husk of speech,
doesn't have to supplant speech. It can fortify it,
or fertilize it. As dead matter, it can either suffo-
cate life or nourish it, kill or invigorate. The important thing is not to lose sight of which should
be in the service of which. Keeping that in mind,
we can accept Socrates' criticism and come out in
defense of the book:

"You're right—if books don't encourage us to
live life to the fullest, they are dead. You're right—
when the miracle of inspired life presents itself, it
would be ridiculous to prefer books. But we no

longer have the leisure of free afternoons in Athens. And the simulacrum of inspired life that exists in the great books seems more than a simulacrum: it seems like life itself, like latent inspiration waiting to be reclaimed. The dead text of Plato's *Dialogues* preserves the germ of your contagious freedom."

Underdeveloped worlds, old and new, have never lacked for founding fathers: people capable of using their skill as speakers to make oases spring up in the cultural desert. The lessons of Socrates—in the form of public discussions, the preaching of missionaries, the teaching of rural schoolmasters, the salons of the great conversationalists—may radiate throughout the community, raising the quality of local life and unleashing its creative possibilities. But thousands of years after writing was invented and centuries after the printing press was introduced, this encouragement doesn't have to be purely oral.

The inertness of the printed word is not a failing of print but a failing of life. There is much dead text in conversation, in the university, in sermons, in speeches, in the words and acts of everyday life. Just consider a medieval scenario that persists to this day: In the classroom, the teacher reads his lecture, and the students take notes. What is the role of the teacher here? Not the Socratic role of the spiritual midwife who guides the intelligence of his interlocutor into the world, but the phonographic role of a needle tracing the written word. Today, when an excess of population, an excess of academicism, and the excessive cost of personal attention make it impossible to have a Socrates in every classroom, at what level is the classroom not an obsolete machine in comparison to other forms of teaching and inspiration, like the library?

Culture is conversation. Writing, reading, editing, printing, distributing, cataloguing, reviewing, can be fuel for that conversation, ways of keeping it lively. It could even be said that to publish a book is to insert it into the middle of a conversation, that to establish a publishing house, bookstore, or library is to start a conversation—a conversation that springs, as it should, from local debate, but that opens up, as it should, to all places and times.

Culture, in the anthropological sense of "way of life," manifests and reproduces itself live, but it is also a collection of works, tools, codes, and repertoires that may or may not be inert text. The same is true of culture in the limited sense of "cultural activities." In both senses, what is important about culture is how alive it is, not how many tons of dead prose it can claim. The Socratic demands of a convivial culture (as Ivan Illich would call it) can be fulfilled, or not, in the agora or in books, the classroom or the library, the café or the bookstore; with recent or medieval technology and in rich or poor communities. The superiority of some cultures or cultural media over others, when it exists, resides in the liveliness or level of vitality they produce, which can only be felt, not measured by statistics. Credentials and statistics are beside the point.

Boredom is the negation of culture. Culture is conversation, liveliness, inspiration. In championing books that matter to us, we can't restrict ourselves to increasing sales, printings, number of titles, news, cultural events, jobs, costs, and all other measurable quantities. The important thing is creative vitality, which we can sense if not measure; it lets us know when we're headed in the right direction, although there are no set rules for encouraging it.

Some examples:

▎ A two-year-old child is at the dinner table with her parents; they are talking to guests in a language that she has never heard before. All of a sudden, she starts to babble, as if she were speaking that language. She wants to participate in the conversation and is confident that she can. In a way, this child is repeating the adventure of learning to talk. And if she lived in the country of the friends who are visiting, she would surely master their language, the same way people learn to swim: by diving right in. Observing this urge to communicate, Paul Goodman believed that children could learn to read spontaneously; that the problem was school, which made them lose the desire. With a grade-school teacher's Socratic irony, he said that if children went to school from the day they were born in order to be taught how to speak, a good percentage of the population would be unable to do so, or would stutter.

▎ A person comes late to a conversation and believes that he can't follow it, that he needs to be better informed: as if knowledge were something other than conversation itself, as if it were something to be acquired elsewhere first. Friends recommend that he take certain classes, which bore him; that he study handbooks, which bore him; that he read the classics, which also bore him. The truly enlightened thing would be to recommend that he have more confidence in his appetite for conversation; to tell him that if he is interested in something he doesn't understand, he should pay more attention, ask questions, reflect, consult dictionaries, manuals, classics, but all in the service of his desire to participate in the ongoing conversation. There is no point in recommending that he try to learn the dictionary from start to finish, systematically, from A to Z. The dictionary, like all study plans, is justified by its use as an aid to conversation, not by its own merits. Naturally, if upon looking up a word he discovers others that interest him, or if upon consulting a classic he finds that his interest goes beyond the matter at hand, he should allow himself to be carried away by curiosity, surprise, astonishment, enjoyment. The desire to follow a conversation that you don't understand is a healthy sign, not an indication of lack of preparation. Discipline is good in the service of desire, not in place of desire. Without desire, there is no living culture.

❚❚ A young writer dreams of writing novels, but feels he isn't ready. He is advised to read the great novelists, but in the originals. He becomes enamored of Dostoyevsky, and twenty years later, instead of a novelist he has become a translator from the Russian. Or he is advised to get his doctorate in literature with a specialty in narrative theory, and twenty years later he isn't a novelist but a professor of semiotics. What one should really say to him is this: What novels have you read that you couldn't put down? Keep reading books like that, and take a look at these others, which might interest you too. What has most excited you to write? Keep writing the same kind of thing, and once you are writing—not before—study the art of writing from the outside, reading this or that book. Don't bury yourself in the history or the theory of the novel without having first fallen under the spell of fiction, without having been seized by the creative thrill of novels.

❚❚ The grandchildren of a forgotten writer have the funds to publish a monumental edition of his complete works. Respect for one's elders may work in the interests of culture, especially when it ensures the care of archives, objects, editions, and all the many other things that might be damaged or lost. It is even more helpful when it facilitates research, with proper or at least careful classification, annotation, indexes, and critical editions. But monuments are designed for ceremonies, not conversation. To incorporate a forgotten writer into a conversation, it is necessary to be familiar with the conversation, to judge where to gain entry and what to introduce; on what subjects and at what time and place to give voice to the forgotten writer; to choose the right text to start people talking. After a few poems, stories, or essays are published in magazines or newspapers, a publishing house (one that conducts the right sort of conversation) should then pick one of his books for publication. And so on, successively, as if he were a living writer, letting one or two years pass between books. This is how writers of other eras, or contemporary writers from other countries, have come to form part of local conversations, gaining access to them by marking their pace and heeding their limitations. Not all conversations are particularly open or intelligent.

▌▎ Many authors send their writing to a publisher without first informing themselves about the character of the house and its list. This is like talking without listening. A friend familiar with the ongoing "conversation" might say this to the writer: "It is useless for you to send this to such-and-such a publisher. Don't you read what he publishes? Your work isn't right for any of his imprints (or any section of his magazine). He just rejected this or that magnificent translation. Why? Because he doesn't publish books in translation. Hadn't you noticed? I hadn't either, but looking through his catalogue, I realized it was true. You can, of course, try the XYZ Institute. Their editorial policy is so amorphous that everything has a place there; but by the same token, you'll be buried in a warehouse, not inserted into an ongoing conversation. You have to find publishers who engage in lively conversations, who have access to readers to whom you really have something to say in the judgment of the publisher. Or somehow you must start a conversation yourself, until the audience you have amassed attracts a publisher."

▮ Juan José Arreola, a man who did much to renew Spanish prose, and a great educator in the Socratic tradition of teaching through conversation, also knew how to use publishing to energize Mexican literature. His legendary small-press series *Los Presentes* led to the formation of a lively circle of young writers who set in motion a number of other initiatives. And he did this with very little material support. Today, when so many institutions possess hundreds of times more resources, it is amazing how few publications and cultural activities make any difference at all. Why is this so? Perhaps because many publishers are not aware that the true art of publishing involves placing the text in the middle of a conversation; knowing how to feed the flames.

This same Arreola coined a publishing maxim: All good publishers have a department of exceptions. But note, exceptions have no meaning when a publisher's list is amorphous. They are only possible when the conversation has an organizing principle. Only at a well-organized table is it possible to see that one of the guests is out of place, that he should be at a different table. The rule of not publishing literature in translation is ridiculous as a general principle, but it gives shape to the conversation of a certain table. Without this coherence, there can be no good publishers, distributors, booksellers, librarians, or reading club and book club administrators.

Culture makes us think in abstract terms, with chaotic results for many endeavors. If we understand culture as a conversation, we can make specific judgments, determining who has something of interest to say to whom, and how, when, and where to bring them together. It helps us to accept that, of everyone in the whole world, the people who will read a new book are so few that a list of them could theoretically be drawn up. The list would be different for each book, of course. In very rare cases, it might be millions of names long, manageable only by the computers of the major book clubs or the big direct-sales companies. But most commonly—in any language—the list is thousands of names long; not even tens of thousands. And just a few thousand copies, read by the right people, are enough to change the course of conversation, the boundaries of literature, and our intellectual life. What sense is there, then, in launching books into infinity so that they are lost in the chaos? With few exceptions, the world of the book has no connection to massive and undifferentiated markets; it relies instead on segmented clienteles, specialized niches, and members of different clubs of enthusiasts. But not all publishers, booksellers, and librarians see the importance of giving shape to these clubs; of making lists of potential readers; of welcoming and facilitating direct contact; of taking into account the tastes and opinions of the participants; of organizing coherent and lively conversations. The success that many small and medium-size houses have had along these lines confirms the idea that organizing the world of books is like organizing a conversation.

Dear Socrates—Phaedrus was right when he remarked on your special talent for inventing Egyptian tales about the origin of writing. But your criticism helps us to identify the true role of books, which is to continue our conversation by other means.

Culture and Commerce

WE WOULD LIKE TO BELIEVE that culture and commerce have nothing to do with each other: that culture circulates and is acquired in noncommercial ways more akin to the cult and the occult; that it is like an initiatory brew given to the chosen to drink; that it is something acquired gradually under the control and with the guarantee of the Establishment.

With our new openness to indigenous cultures, the picture is complicated but doesn't change. Although it is said, and seemingly with great daring, that these cultures are as valid as our own, the separation is maintained by the fact that they are "other"; when they stop being "other," they are "commercialized." Culture is the otherness possessed by "cultured" people and by indigenous groups still on the margins of the cultural metropolis. The intermediate zones—radio songs, soap operas, and even traditional folkloric perform-ances—are commercial productions, not culture.

In all of this, some people assume that business is dirty, or at least, not very noble. For them it is repugnant, for example, that commerce should be associated with the divine. But what of Hermes, inventor of the lyre, god of commerce, roads, and communication, a great figure in the annals of alchemy? The word *commerce* had, and still has, non-economic meanings. For one of them— "Intercourse or converse with God, with spirits, passions, thoughts, etc."—the OED quotes Wordsworth: "We sank each into commerce with his private thoughts." Of course, that meant silence and meditation, not the marketing of ideas. In 1850, thoughts, ideas, knowledge, were not considered products. Even in 1962, when Fritz Machlup published *The Production and Distribution of Knowledge in the United States,* he had to justify the strange project of measuring knowledge in the Gross National Product. By trying to include the value of books, media, education, research, information machines, and information services (from 23 to 32 percent of GNP in 1958, depending on the method of measurement) as part of the total GNP, he had to put a dollar value on what had previously been considered beyond pricing. For thousands of years, knowledge was assumed to come from heaven and to be shared by initiation, in a "commerce" outside the market. The transmission of knowledge "from mouth to ear" was normal in medieval guilds, Freemason societies, closed-shop unions, esoteric circles, and even good manners.

To say that something was learned at the breast means that it was transferred in natural commerce, that it wasn't acquired with money or lessons, let alone independent reading. According to this tradition, knowledge that is sold or publicized is degraded, commercialized.

Note also the ambivalence or duplicity with which success (exoteric, external, commercial) is desired and feared in cultural circles, and the importance of gaining the respect of a small group over and above that of the public. To ignore the public is, ultimately, the actual negation of culture: a failure to communicate, but also salvation from the perdition of commerce and success, a guarantee of purity. Commercial success can be counterproductive, leading to a loss of credibility in the best circles. We want books to be democratic objects, to be read by everyone, to be everywhere accessible, but we also want them to continue to be sacred.

There is in these ambivalences a single more fundamental one—an ambivalence of the thing itself. Culture isn't a product, of course. But what then are oranges, orchids, birds, sunsets? Anything can begin as revelation and become currency, an object, a commodity. To avoid this, a process of certification is invented, as ambiguous as the object itself. The word becomes a notarized contract; the academic title provides a guarantee; the institution legitimizes; the stamp of the cognoscenti certifies.

And therein lies the contradiction. Modern culture was born with the printing revolution. Rejecting traditional mediation, it thrives on independent revelation: the reading of the thing itself revealing its meaning to the reader. But the state we call "cultured" continues to mean something entirely different, something dependent on a process unrelated to reading: on the rites of passage of an institution that consecrates, certifies, and guarantees. Truly modern developments—free reading and commercial publishing—seem now less cultured than does the possession of scholarly knowledge, still hierarchic as in medieval times. Can there be such a thing as noncommercial commerce? According to anthropologists, it has always existed. Trade began as dialogue: Tribal exchange (before the advent of barter or buying and selling) was the give and take of conversation. And so it is still, as is certainly evident in the attitude of locals who refuse to sell to those they don't like or those who won't banter or bargain. They do not think of themselves as vending machines; they are not exchanging things for money, mechanically, but engaging in dialogue. If engineers could disassemble a vending machine, go back to its remote anthropological origin, and get the basic blueprint, they would find a miracle saying, "Good Morning." This is the way trade in monasteries once worked, too, and even the selling of indulgences, which may be seen as contradictory in a way that reveals the ambiguity of any commodity. Isn't selling flowers like selling a miracle, or grace, or passports to heaven? Isn't it like putting a price tag on eternity? The consciousness of this ambiguity arose at the same time as commercial culture, which was scandalized by the sale of indulgences, but couldn't turn back to feudal self-sufficiency.

This kind of guilty conscience undermines the book business and all businesses that consider themselves above business (communes, cooperatives, parish stores, union stores, state-run stores). The business of books both derives from and distances itself from the temple; it grew alongside the commercial revolution and prefigured the industrial revolution (the book was one of the first manufactured items to be made cheaper by standardization); it favors the kind of independent revelation championed by Protestantism (which abolished the selling of indulgences, but made the Bible a bestseller) and also the French Revolution, which, some might say, began with the sale of encyclopedias (Robert Darnton, *The Business of Enlightenment: A Publishing History of the* Encyclopédie *1775–1800*).

An assignment for the reader: investigate why the French Encyclopedists, as revolutionaries, spoke up for free trade; and how it is that liberal culture, the independent professions, and the printed book emerged at the same time. Consider the progress of the cultural revolution from the invention of the printing press to Protestantism, and the resulting counterrevolution, which restored new forms of clericalism: professional schools, Freemasonry, the Communist party, the pretension of teaching everything academically, state intervention, the pressure of the great bureaucracies (public, union, academic, and private) on independent life. See in the disdain for business the reactionary abomination of the horrors of freedom—a contradiction of the commercial origins of modern culture.

All commerce is conversation: in other words, it is culture, always at the risk of becoming blah-blah-blah. It's all very well to feel that books are not a commodity, but dialogue and revelation; instead of leading to the rejection of commerce, however, this should make us realize that in the end nothing is just a commodity.

Some Questions About the Circulation of Books

THREE COMMON ASSUMPTIONS about the circulation of books:

ılı The book was the first means of mass communication to arise in history, and it continues to be the greatest.

ılı The influence of books is enormous: culture spreads and is communicated through the book.

ılı It is because books are expensive — especially for the masses in poor countries — that they are not more widely available.

Are books one of the mass media? The comparison of books with other means of mass communication is understandable for a number of reasons: they may sell millions of copies; they are intended for an anonymous public; they are an industrial product that reproduces and multiplies symbols; historically, they are at the beginning of the line that may be traced from the Gutenberg Bible of the fifteenth century to the radio, film, television, and digital media of the twenty-first century. But a distinction must be made.

Networks of surface mail, telegraph, telephone, and electronic mail, even though they are massive, exist primarily for the purpose of direct communication between two correspondents. On the other hand, oral texts like the *Iliad* and the *Odyssey* and books in manuscript or print form are something very different, the forerunners of the organs of mass communication: they send signals from a central point to the public. They are not a medium of exchange; they are aimed at an anonymous public. That is why it is natural to make the comparison. However, these various comparisons lead to misunderstandings harmful to the book since they imply that the other media have superseded the book, technologically, in mass appeal, and in influence. Therefore, the book must be defended against the new media—with complaints about the way prices and distribution prevent mass circulation and with affirmations of the book's greatness and ultimate influence despite all obstacles.

That the book is the precursor of the mass media and that it doesn't have the same reach seems to put it at fault, and gives rise to false problems and false solutions.

It is worth asking, in the first place, whether all books need or deserve a mass readership. The immense majority of books are not written for large audiences, nor do they need them in order to make money. At the other extreme, some bad books reach huge audiences, comparable to or larger than those reached by the press, radio, or television, though this in no way makes them any less bad.

Books are not really one of the mass media, though they can play the role of one without thereby providing any special advantage to society. Of course, we derive a social advantage when many of us have read a few of the same books, especially if those books are the classics—it aids conversation. Shared knowledge of the alphabet, numbers, weights and measures, vocabulary, and a minimum of references is a good thing—it allows us to understand one another. Some common knowledge of texts, songs, sayings, news stories, and films is also a good thing—without it, conversation would be impossible. Uniformity is boring and numbing, but absolute differentiation isolates us. In order for diversity to be enriching, a common base of knowledge is required. Beyond that, variety is preferable. What is desirable is not that all books should have millions of readers, but that they should attain their natural readership—the readership they might have in a perfect world where distribution was flawless and price not an issue, giving every possible interested reader the opportunity to read them.

Is the book a means of action? It is worth asking ourselves, too, about the influence of books. It is clear that such influence exists, but not how it works, or how powerful or good or bad it is.

The traditional hypothesis is evangelical in form: The seed is cast, and some is lost or falls on sterile ground, or is smothered, or gives little fruit; but a few chosen souls respond by transforming their lives and the lives of others, propagating the influence. This is how ideas are spread, especially if they manage to reach the people in power, or if the people with the ideas come to power. So it happens that a dialogue or tradition is established through space and time, and a few books by Aristotle stamp their character on the European languages and shape the mental habits of millions who have never even read Aristotle. So it happens that this same dialogue becomes tangled up in landmark events and allows us to see, as in the Hegel-Marx-Castro progression, the ways in which a powerful intellectual influence secretly shapes history.

All of this is a pleasant consolation, especially for those authors who sell few copies of their books and are able to think to themselves that, after all, Hegel sold even fewer. But it may be no more than that—a way of banishing the nightmare of the opposite hypothesis, which hasn't been proved either but is no less widespread: that to write is to situate oneself on the margins of reality. Socrates didn't believe in the importance of writing. Rimbaud and Juan Rulfo gave up writing. Many churchmen and revolutionaries have felt guilty or narcissistic for submerging themselves in an activity (writing) so remote from practical results. The guilty feelings of those who write are well known, and they partly explain our obsession with putting the pen at the service of "worthy causes" in order to feel less useless. If Latin American universities could wait until 1966 for the translation of *Phenomenology of Spirit* without collapsing for want of Hegel, and if very few revolutionary students ever read the book, and if Castro publicly declares that he never read more than the beginning of *Capital,* what do we mean when we talk about the influence of books, never mind on the masses?

It is necessary to distinguish among and judge separately a cluster of different phenomena associated with the so-called influence of books. The fame of authors or titles is one thing, the actual sales of copies is another, the reading of them is another, and the assimilation and diffusion of their content is yet another; we must also consider the causal connections between the preceding phenomena (renown, sales, reading, assimilation, diffusion) and what we are able to observe of the public's behavior.

One can be known as a writer despite never having written a book; or if the book has actually been written, despite its not selling; or if it is sold, then despite its not being read; or if it has been read, then despite its failure to change anything. One can sell many books and not be particularly famous. Or one can wield considerable influence without having written much at all. These are related, but very different, phenomena.

And all have yet to be studied. Is politically engaged poetry really good for anything? Does pornographic literature really do any harm? If those who committed suicide after reading *The Sorrows of Young Werther* had never read the book, would they have killed themselves anyway? Did the reading of Marx cause the events of July 26 in Cuba? Did the reading of the Gospels lead to the bombing of Hiroshima?

We can commission studies that allow us to measure and codify readership by city neighborhoods, income, age, sex, habits, preferences, and so on. But it isn't easy to measure influence. We assume that advertisers have no interest in studying whether television is bad for children, and in what ways. But on subjects that *are* of interest to them, like the influence of advertising on sales, they haven't achieved much precision either. The Viscount of Leverhulme, founder of the soap empire Lever Brothers, made a joke that is still in circulation today: "Half the money I spend on advertising is wasted, and the trouble is I don't know which half" (David Ogilvy, *Confessions of an Advertising Man*).

Regarding books, our ignorance is greater. In the absence of studies, there exist a series of pious theories: no book is so bad that it has no redeeming qualities; any book is better than any television program; there is nothing nobler than raising a child, planting a tree, or writing a book.

Believing in books as a means of action or not believing in them is first and foremost precisely that: a matter of belief.

Which masses don't read? There is an essential economic difference between the book, as a medium, and the other media. It is the business of the press, radio, and television to gather an audience that can be sold to a third party. The content, which must be acceptable to that third party (the advertiser), serves as bait to attract and determine the size and type of audience that the newspaper, radio, or television company can deliver. Obviously, a manufacturer of power shovels has no interest in buying the audience that television has to offer. Television can get millions of people to watch a boxing match, but very few of those viewers will be interested in buying power shovels. The right venue for assembling such a limited audience, at a reasonable cost, is a magazine that specializes in subjects of interest to the construction industry.

This explains why some specialized magazines are distributed free to readers whose description fits the profile of the target audience. The money the magazine makes from subscriptions might be so small that the publisher prefers to discount it and increase the magazine's true income, which comes from selling advertisements, by offering advertisers a more select, more profitable, and better-packaged audience.

In the management of many sports stadiums, the difference between losing and making money depends on the proper design of the passageways for the optimum circulation of vendors. The sporting event is thus a way of assembling an audience that may be sold to hotdog, beer, popcorn, and coffee concessions.

In the case of the book, there are no third parties: all costs are paid by the consumer. Where commercial broadcast radio and television are concerned, the opposite is true: the audience pays for nothing except the purchase of the equipment. Newspapers and magazines are paid for partly by third parties and partly by the customer.

It follows, therefore, that for the reader books are relatively more expensive than the other media. The book's relative expense limits its reach, especially when its potential readers aren't well off, though public libraries reduce this barrier by providing access to books for free. The main obstacle to the circulation of books is not price, but the different interests of the author and the reader, the properties of the text, and the difficulties of reading and writing. Even supposing that everyone in the world were interested in metallurgy or surrealism, there would be books on surrealism and metallurgy that some people would not be able to follow without certain preliminary studies. These difficulties enormously reduce a book's readership, no matter how cheap it is.

The world isn't waiting with bated breath to buy and read anyone's latest masterpiece, even if it deals with metallurgy, surrealism, or some other subject of central importance to the human species. But if it were not for the more-or-less narcissistic illusion of feeling ourselves the center of a whole that cries out for us, how would any of us ever write, when faced with all the statistical evidence discouraging it? If we consider the gravity of the problems of the Third World, and the importance of agricultural productivity in solving those problems; if we consider that, as Santayana said, those who cannot remember the past are condemned to repeat it; and if we are aware of the historical persistence of the fetishization of farming implements, how is it not possible to see the importance of *The History and Structure of the Myths of Fire-Stick Farming Among the Southern Bororos*?

No author believes his book is anything but essential, because to focus properly on his subject he must see his work as the center of a whole. But how can the reader gain a sense of the whole from all the many centers that demand his attention? Unless he is equipped with similar background and interests, it is difficult. A book is like a conversation, and it isn't true that anyone can follow each and every conversation, joining or abandoning it at will. For that to be possible, we'd always have to be discussing the weather, or something similar, in a conversation destined to begin over and over again and never move on. To get anywhere, and especially certain difficult places, it is necessary to accumulate a minimum of "flight hours" in common.

The problem is not that millions of poor people have little or no buying power. You may have the money to buy a book but not the interest or the training to follow its content. This happens even with college graduates. Many of them would rather write than read. In fact, millions of them have never learned what it is to love to read.

Learning to read is the integration of units of ever-more-complex meaning:

▮▮ The integration of the letters that make up a word. With our alphabet and our standard teaching methods, a first stage is to learn to see a word at a glance. This isn't particularly easy, nor is it a task just for children. It's as difficult as reading Chinese or hieroglyphics. The difference between spelling something out and seeing it at a glance is enormous, and the latter skill isn't acquired without practice. You may instantly register the word "electromotive" without realizing how the child who sounds it out must go back to the beginning and start over, because by the time he gets to "t" he has lost the whole he was piecing together, letter by letter. But the same thing happens when you learn another alphabet (as an effort separate from learning another language); the Greek or Gothic alphabet, for example. If you've taken classes in German using the Roman alphabet, and then are faced with German in Gothic script, the words you knew lose their typographic transparency, bristle with visual complications, and are lost in the spiny foliage of Gothic characters; you must spell them out.

To spell words out is to recognize each letter as a separate whole, with a potential for assimilation into the greater whole that encompasses and modifies it: it is a search for tentative wholes that may be satisfactorily integrated under specific conditions; a search through the tangle of excessive proximity for the forest lost among the trees; it is a move away from the silence of the letter (whose barely perceptible slip into meaning we've learned to see thanks to the lessons of Concrete Poetry) toward the miracle of the full word.

▐▐ Next, all the words in a sentence must be integrated. The whole process is repeated on a second level. Words, with their thousands of possible connotations, can also be mute, and wall themselves off as discrete entities. Here integration is more complex, because the contextual modulations (without even taking into account yet the context of the sentence) have typographical, prosodic, syntactical, and semantic complications that impose more restrictions on the integration of units of meaning.

Historically, reading began as a simple recovery of oral discourse, which was recorded in a graphic code, just as a secretary takes dictation of a letter in shorthand code, in order to reconstruct it. People didn't read to understand, but to hear, and through hearing comprehend. It was sound that was recovered from writing first, and then meaning. Just as children take time to learn to read without sounding words out, it took humanity time to learn to read silently, to grasp the meaning of writing directly without converting it into sound. According to Plutarch, Alexander was able to read silently; seven centuries later, Saint Augustine still marveled at having seen Saint Ambrose do the same thing.

▐▌ And so on, until it is possible to read a paragraph, which is as far as many literate people get. Adults may be capable of juggling relatively difficult and complex units of oral expression, but incapable of keeping the same balls in the air as they read a text silently. Sometimes, the effort is communal: a peasant who knows how to read transforms the paragraphs of a newspaper story into an intelligible oral version, and the story is then grasped in its entirety by those who are listening. The reader pauses at intervals because he also needs to listen; he needs his own oral version, without which he is unable to understand what the newspaper reports. He "sounds out" paragraphs, de-paragraphing them, if that term may be permitted, and like a child, he can reach "z" without comprehending the article in its totality. He needs to amass the whole, paragraph by paragraph, like the child who reads letter by letter.

▐▌ The next level—which many doctors, engineers, teachers, and researchers, still "sounding words out" like the peasants of the previous example, never reach—is to grasp a book all at once, in its entirety. How can anyone who labors painstakingly over a period of days, weeks, and months, or who forgets the meaning of the whole by the time "z" is reached, read a book? And how many college classes are no more than the tortuous reading of a text over the course of a year? Is anything more certain to make a book completely unintelligible than reading it slowly enough? It's like examining a mural from two centimeters away and scanning it at a rate of ten square centimeters every third day for a year, like a shortsighted slug. This doesn't allow for the integration of the whole, for taking in the mural at a glance.

And then years go by, and professional experience and life experience cause people to mature, even in their relationship to language, and one encounters college-educated people who perform with reasonable skill in the workplace and are capable of carrying on a conversation of some sophistication, but who pick up a book and know no better than to hug the ground, dragging themselves laboriously through foliage that, from their slug's perspective, they are unable to rapidly survey.

And how many people want to feel like slugs, especially once they know what it is like to express themselves intelligently in conversation? This natural dissatisfaction accentuates the difference between the "developed" oral side and the "underdeveloped" written side; it relegates the reading of books to a vicious cycle of stagnation. People who feel this way don't read books. They never really learned to read books. Reading never appealed to them. They never acquired a taste for reading, and so they will never enjoy it. And, of course, it isn't necessary to read in order to be successful in a career, to be accepted socially, or to make money.

Those who do read books because they were lucky enough to have had parents or teachers or friends who were readers, those few, even, who read a book a day with the unfettered voracity that later tends to embarrass them — not realizing that this very habit has taught them to read, since it is reading at such a pace that teaches the reader to see the whole at a glance — are so few and far between that average book reading is low, even in developed countries. Reading is not the act of spelling out words, or the effort of dragging oneself across the surface of a mural that will never be viewed in its entirety. Beyond the alphabet, the paragraph, and the short article which may still be taken in all at once, there are functional illiteracies of the book. The great barrier to the free circulation of books is the mass of privileged citizens who have college degrees but never learned to read properly, despite the excellent guides that exist, for example, Mortimer Adler's *How to Read a Book* and Daniel Pennac's *Better than Life.*

Statistics published by UNESCO make it evident that the explosion in the number of books published in the twentieth century parallels the proliferation of academic degrees. But the explosion says more about supply than demand. College graduates are more interested in publishing books than reading them.

Publishing is a standard part of establishing an academic or bureaucratic career. It is like writing the necessary reports or properly filling out the forms required to enter a competition. It has nothing to do with reading or writing. Reading is difficult, it takes time away from the pursuit of a career, and it doesn't gain anyone points except in lists of works cited. Publishing is a means to an end. Reading is useless: it is a vice, pure pleasure.

The End of the Book

NO EXPERTS IN TECHNOLOGICAL forecasting are predicting the end of fire or the wheel or the alphabet, inventions that are thousands of years old but have never been surpassed, despite being the products of underdeveloped peoples. And yet there are prophets who proclaim the death of the book. This prophesy is understood as an apocalyptic judgment: the overabundance of books oppresses humanity and in the end will provoke divine wrath. But as a technological judgment, it doesn't withstand the slightest scrutiny.

Books can be skimmed. In this sense, only paintings are superior to books.

A film or television show, although it is visual, cannot be taken in at a glance, like a painting. Nor can it be skimmed. It is possible to lose concentration and be distracted, but not to move ahead to see what comes next, flip backward to understand something better, or pause for a moment to think.

Programs recorded on videocassettes or DVDs do allow the viewer to scroll back and forth, but exploring them isn't easy. Not even the fastest computer is able to give the sense of the whole that a quick scan of a book gives, and with the same ease. One becomes impatient exploring the files of a computer; it isn't easy to get a quick idea of the content.

It is very difficult to get a rapid sense of a temporal sequence (even if it is visual) that must pass through a machine. In order to follow what comes out of a player piano, record player, tape player, film projector, radio, television, videocassette player, computer, telephone, or fax, you must pay close attention to the sequence of images or sounds. To search for something, it is necessary to proceed blindly, stubbornly, clumsily, without being able to see any distance ahead.

It is easier to find things in books—which is ironic, after Marshall McLuhan's declaration of the obsolescence of "linear writing." Nothing requires more "linear reading" than television, tapes, and records. Unlike books (or paintings), they can't be taken in all at once. They hearken back to the texts of antiquity, like the Dead Sea Scrolls, which had to be rolled from one rod to the other in order to be read.

This new-media disadvantage is evident even in direct-mail advertising. A reader may give a printed pamphlet two seconds of attention before he discards it, but there is less chance that the recipient of an unsolicited CD will load and consider it: that would take more than two seconds. Similarly, even at the height of the paperless era, many people performing office tasks prefer to work with printouts rather than onscreen files. But most ironic of all is the printed instruction booklet that comes with so-called cutting-edge electronic equipment. No book requires electronic instructions explaining how to read it.

The great advantage of an electronic text is the speed at which words (or subjects, if they are previously catalogued—like those listed in the indexes of books—and are requested correctly and specifically) may be searched for. This is especially true of CDs and DVDs, which allow readers to view lists of words and subjects on the screen before searching for the corresponding texts. When there are no lists available, whether because they weren't created or because consulting them is difficult (downloading a thesaurus from the Internet can take hours) the advantage is greatly lessened: in a blind search, the reader has to guess which words will generate useful responses. But even with the help of lists, it is impossible to skim electronic texts.

A book is read at a pace determined by the reader. With the new media, a reader has to adapt to the pace set by a machine. And "reading" can only be undertaken at one speed. A disc, tape, or film whose speed is altered is no longer legible. In contrast, books (within certain limits) can be read at the speed required by the reader, mood, purpose, or landscape of the text or the circumstances.

This is a significant freedom. A book can be explored at thousands of words per minute with speed-reading techniques, or one revelatory line can be lingeringly contemplated. And it is so easy to turn back, to reread, to halt, to skip things that are of no interest. With the new media, these can be cumbersome operations.

Books are portable. The advantage of the book is that all the other media require two steps to be read: one step to transform the mechanical, magnetic, optical, or electronic signal (received or taped) into something that in turn (the second step) is legible by a human being. Whereas the book is directly legible. It doesn't require that you carry an intermediary reader, supposedly portable and hardly private, that obliges your neighbors to participate in something that is of no interest to them. Nor does it need to be taken somewhere special, where the machine will work. A book can be read almost anywhere and in any position, whether the reader is standing up, sitting down, or lying in bed.

There is no advantage whatsoever to reading novels on a screen that is barely portable and displays text of minimal contrast and primitive typography. There may be an advantage to reading reference books on screen, especially if the electronic version is equipped with supplementary files and programs. An encyclopedia that allows you to read an article on the hummingbird, hear its trill, see color pictures of it in flight and at rest, read all the references to the hummingbird in other articles, and see and hear the name of the hummingbird in other languages has obvious advantages over the printed version. And a disc is more portable, or so it would seem. The true comparison, however, isn't between the many volumes of an encyclopedia and a single disc, but between the encyclopedia and a complete set of electronic equipment that is not solely dedicated to the reading of that disc. In practice, for rapid consultations it may be more work to get the disc, bring it to the machine (if it is not being used by someone else), and turn the machine on or switch from one program to another than to pick up the printed volume and consult it directly.

Perhaps modern technology's greatest tribute to the advantages of the age-old book is the attempt to develop electronic screens as thin and flexible as paper, hundreds of which could be bound into something like a book, which would have the same visual and typographic appearance as a book and even the same tactile feel, without electric or electronic cords: e-book readers disguised as printed books.

You don't need to make an appointment to read a book. To see a television show, you must be free at a certain time, or program your video-cassette recorder. The spectator must match his schedule to the program schedule. In contrast, the book molds itself to the schedule of the reader: it is available when and where he wants it. It doesn't require a previous appointment.

People change channels easily, and that habit of surfing may be considered a kind of freedom when compared to the cinema and especially to plays and concerts, which are social ceremonies requiring fixed attention in formal circumstances. In extreme cases, attendance requires an invitation, coordination with other people, security precautions, special attire, and preparations for a full-fledged excursion—in order to arrive somewhere at a certain time where you may not be distracted, eat or drink, record the proceedings, leave before the show is over, or avoid paying a high cost in time, money, and respect for others, even if the performance is terrible—all of which is justified only in special cases. But television zapping is nothing compared to book zapping, which offers more variety (you don't need a big library in order to have access to more books than television channels) and more flexibility time-wise. It allows you to zap forward and back; it preserves information (without obliging you to record anything); and it doesn't require a previous appointment. The very ease of jumping back and forth within a book or hopping from one book to another prompted Seneca to warn Lucilius of its peril: the dissipation of the reader.

Books are cheap. They are so cheap that private ownership, and even private publication, is relatively easy. Millions of readers can afford to buy a collection of great books, but not an equivalent collection of paintings. A person of modest resources can pay to have a book of his own published, but not to stage an opera or produce a film he has written.

Books are so cheap that we talk about selling them as if the only desirable option were the personal library. We don't think about museums that way. On the contrary, private museums are considered a luxury (and sometimes viewed askance).

Television and the press are so expensive that they can't even be paid for directly by the public; they are funded by advertisers. Film, the press, and television require audiences of hundreds of thousands in order to be cost-effective. Books, with no advertisements inside, are paid for by a few thousand readers. No cheaper means to address so few people — so widely dispersed in place and time — has ever been invented.

Books permit greater variety. Producing a television show for three million people justifies an enormous budget. If the same audience were divided among six channels, the variety would increase by a factor of six, but budgets would be strained because each program would have to cost only one-sixth as much. If it were divided among a thousand channels, the variety would be a thousand times greater, but the budgeting would be impossible: you can't produce television shows for three thousand people.

This explains why television is disappointing: because it has to appeal to hundreds of thousands or millions of people. The ideal situation — in television as well as books — is for something truly excellent to appeal to a large public. This happens from time to time. But in the case of books, if it doesn't happen it doesn't spell financial disaster, as it does with television. Television must produce bestsellers: good, bad, or excellent.

Books, on the other hand, can be bestsellers, but they don't have to be. It is economically feasible to publish an excellent book even if it doesn't interest more than three or four thousand people, and many bestsellers have gotten their start that way. Octavio Paz's *Labyrinth of Solitude,* which has sold more than a million copies in its various editions, was first issued in a small printing and wasn't reissued for nine years. If it had been a television program, it would never have been produced.

The Cost of Reading

IF A MASS MARKET PAPERBACK costs ten dollars and takes two hours to read, for a minimum wage earner the time spent is worth as much as the book. For college graduates earning fifty to five hundred dollars an hour, the cost of buying and reading the book is one hundred to one thousand dollars. And that doesn't include the cost of getting to know about the book, looking for it, going to buy it or ordering it, paying for it, covering the shipping expenses, tracking the order, making a return package if necessary, finding a place to read it, and reserving shelf space for it.

Nobel Prize-winning economist Ronald H. Coase introduced the concept of transaction costs. Processing a bank check (writing it, keeping the record, protecting it, mailing it, cashing it, verifying the balance, accounting for the transaction by all the firms and banks involved, writing and auditing the statements) may cost several dollars, whether the check is for one dollar or one million dollars. You may ignore transaction costs when the check is big but not when the check is small.

Books are so inexpensive that the handling of them carries costs out of proportion to the size of the transaction. The cost of the attention given to a single title or a single copy can be greater than the expected income. This may explain the desire to handle only high-volume titles or high-volume orders, but the practical solution is to devise means of handling transactions adapted to small orders. This applies to every stage of the process, from design to lending by librarians. Take, for instance, promotion and advertising: If you allow for 4 percent on sales, what can you do for most titles? Not much. Your budget is equivalent to 120 copies for each 3,000 copies to be sold. After giving away review and other complimentary copies, you are left on a shoestring. Spending a lot on promotion and advertising makes sense only for bestsellers—if you are sure you have one.

The cost of printing a book is not a major factor in the cost of reading. To print an extra copy of a mass paperback may cost a dollar (this is the marginal, not the average cost). So when readers pay ten dollars, the price is already ten times the marginal printing cost, essentially because of all the handling involved in transferring the manuscript from author to editor and the finished copies from printer to bookseller. Nor is this the end. Just finding and keeping interesting books is very expensive, for readers and librarians.

In 1989, the British Library, which receives free copies of all the books published in the United Kingdom, complained that receiving them, cataloging them, exhibiting them, and properly caring for them cost fifty pounds per copy, plus one pound per copy per year. This was more than the average price of the books. From this perspective, it is easy to understand the complaints of the Mexican writer Alfonso Reyes, who came to feel himself a slave of his own library and of the infinite number of complimentary copies of books received from authors and publishers; or the writer who gives his collection away in exchange for receiving library services for the books he has donated; or the writer who decides not to create a library, saying, "I will keep only the books I plan to read. Those I've already read (or will never read), I will discard."

Time is by far the most expensive aspect of reading, excepting time spent in certain circumstances: in transit, ill health, prison, or retirement. In a wealthy economy, time is worth more than things, and it is easier to buy things than to find the time to enjoy them. To purchase books that one will never read is understandable: we think we might read them one day, and in the meantime, they can be shown off to visitors or mentioned in conversation. Reading is a luxury of the poor, the sick, prisoners, retirees, students. As students become young executives with overcrowded schedules, and as their salaries rise, reading (if it is not required) becomes a luxury for them, too.

Writing well also becomes a luxury because it requires more time of the writer. If he is in prison or retired, he has plenty of free time, but not if he is a doctor, a lawyer, or an executive. He can't devote himself to rewriting a paragraph over and over, although the additional work might save his readers time.

It is absurd for the writer to devote two hours to saving his reader a minute if the text is a note to his secretary. But if it is a book with twelve thousand readers, each minute represents a social benefit of two hundred hours in exchange for two, and the reward is one hundred times the cost. It would make sense for a portion of that reward to go to the writer who has taken the trouble to write well, and to the publisher who prints such a readable book—but it isn't easy to charge for the effort.

The cost of reading would be much reduced if authors and publishers respected readers' time more, and if texts that had little to say, or were badly written or poorly edited, were never published.

The Supply and Demand of Poetry

FROM TIME TO TIME, a book of poems becomes a bestseller. In 1987, a young schoolteacher and translator of classic Japanese named Machi Tawara published *Sarada kinenbi* (*Salad Anniversary*), a collection of tanka that has sold more than three million copies in Japan. Thirteen years later, *Beowulf: A New Verse Translation* by Seamus Heaney became a bestseller with hundreds of thousands of copies in print. The general experience, however, is that books of poetry sell no more than a few hundred copies.

According to the American Booksellers Association, sales of poetry rise in April, when National Poetry Month is celebrated and some hundred businesses support this promotion of the American Academy of Poets in two hundred thousand schools, libraries, and bookstores. But in April 1997, this translated into only $137,000 worth of sales for the chain store Borders Books & Music, one of the sponsors. In the face of such meager demand, the supply is impressive. *Poetry*, the respected magazine founded in 1912, celebrated by T. S. Eliot, and fortunate enough to have a circulation of ten thousand copies (ten times the average for poetry magazines), currently receives ninety thousand submissions a year from all over the world.

One understands the bleak picture painted by Carl J. Buchanan ("How to Publish Poems Today," aboutthearts.com/poetspage.htm, October 2, 2002): "An entire nation submitting to a handful of 'real' journals gives rise to literary congestion of hitherto unheard-of proportions. . . . Today, versus 1980, there is a vast, at least a twenty-fold increase, in the number of poems submitted." But there is no need to feel nostalgic for the nineteen-seventies, when *Coda: Poets and Writers Newsletter* reported that the *New Yorker* was publishing three poems a week, but receiving eight hundred submissions. *Coda* also reported a frankly disturbing incentive advertised by the Golden Quill Poetry Book Club: the offer to include in *The Golden Quill Anthology* a poem by every subscriber who bought at least five books a year.

The terrible thing about this policy is that it makes the problem painfully clear: As the university-educated population grows, it is not so much the number of those who read that increases but the number of those who want to be read. The rule instituted by Golden Quill goes to show that not even poets buy poetry, unless they are required to do so in order to see their own work published.

Ploughshares once complained that it was receiving sixteen thousand manuscripts a year from some six thousand people, of whom not even two hundred were subscribers. Each time it published an advertisement soliciting subscriptions, it got ten or fifteen submissions for each subscription ordered. Nevertheless, it rejected the practice adopted by some journals, which refused to read the letters of prospective writers unless they were subscribers.

If all those who wanted to be read would actually read, there would be an unprecedented boom, because never have so many millions of people dreamed of being published. But the hardly pleasant narcissism of "read me and I'll read you" has degenerated into a narcissism that isn't even reciprocal: Don't ask me to pay attention to you; pay attention to *me*. I don't have the time or the money or the desire to read what you've written; I want *your* time, *your* money, *your* desire. Never mind your concerns; what about mine?

The poet Judson Jerome once said that if writers were truly considerate, they would place a five-dollar bill in each book they put into circulation, in symbolic recognition of the time they were asking of their readers and friends. This is a rational solution in a market economy: if supply exceeds demand and no one is forced to buy, prices will drop until they fall below zero, and writers will have to pay rather than charge to be read.

A welfare state solution would see the creation of a national corps of literary geishas, with degrees in literature and the psychology of writers. They would work full time with the writers whom no one read, listening to them, reading their work, praising them, and consoling them.

Another solution might be rationing. A National Regulatory Board of Supply and Demand could establish a system whereby those who wanted their work read would have to register and prove that they had done some reading themselves. For each thousand poems (or stories or articles or books) read, a petitioner would have the right to publish one poem (or story or article or book). The prescribed ratio would be constantly adjusted until supply was in equilibrium with demand.

A Hair Shirt for
Masochistic Authors

CONSIDER EVERYTHING that could be done for a book! Television, press, radio; government, businesses, universities, libraries; criticism, conferences, friends; bookstores, department stores, pharmacies, airports, newspaper stands, book clubs, mail order, door-to-door sales, telephone sales, installment sales; the world market, translations; theater, film, radio, and television adaptations . . .

Yes, there is much that could be done. And all of it is done, with impressive results, for the Bible; all of it has been done for Mao's *Little Red Book*. But is it possible to do everything for every book?

To begin with, "possible" has a cruelly physical sense. How many books fit in a bookstore? Thousands in a small store; twenty thousand in an average store; hundreds of thousands in a very few giant stores. All in all, a tiny percentage of the total number for sale.

How many books fit in a reader's house? Not many. And readers never get rid of the books they've already read, or are never going to read, to make room for others; it would make them feel bad.

How many commercials are shown on television? A few thousand different ones a year. If a commercial were made for every book, there would be no time to show each one, even if all the other commercials, soap operas, newscasts, and every other program were eliminated.

Let's say that, under the sponsorship of UNESCO, the best critics in the world were hired so that every single book published got exactly one review—one brilliant review. And let's suppose that each review was no more than three pages long. This system would produce enough material for the publication of ten thousand books a year, composed solely of reviews. (Let's also say—for the sake of the world's long-suffering readers—that these collections themselves would never be reviewed, although such self-abnegation would be a lot to ask of ten thousand great critics— if so many could indeed be found.)

Most books are never reviewed, never translated, never reissued. They are sold (if they sell), as novelties, but after the small initial sale, there is no second wave of sales. They may be found (if they are to be found at all) in the libraries of friends, on some bookstore remainder tables, or in a few bibliographical listings—not in the Annals of History.

And yet we keep writing books.

Dante-esque calculations have been made concerning the growth rate of the earth's population, predicting, for example, the year that the earth will become standing room only. Nevertheless, about 100 million children are born each year—many times fewer than the number of books printed! Which kind of overpopulation poses a greater threat to humanity? Which kind of reproduction is more irresponsible? The kind that seeks to perpetuate a name through children or through books?

Your book is a scrap of paper that blows about in the streets, litters cities, piles up in the trash bins of the planet. It is cellulose, and cellulose it will become.

Constellations of Books

A READER WHO READS carefully, reflects, engages in lively conversation with other readers, remembers, and rereads can become acquainted with a thousand books in a lifetime. A prodigious or professional reader, who handles and consults books with specific intent, can read perhaps several times as many, rarely more. But there are millions of books for sale, dozens of millions in libraries, and uncounted millions of unpublished manuscripts. There are more books to contemplate than stars in a night on the high seas. In this immensity, how is a reader to find his personal constellation, those books that will put his life in communication with the universe? And how is a single book among the millions to find its readers?

Friendship between a reader and a book may spring from a fortunate accident and extend itself to other books mentioned by the author. Or it may come from the recommendation of a friend, a teacher, or parents, who convey their own enthusiasm or encourage the enthusiasm of the young reader ("If you liked that book, you may like these others"), or from the stimulating effect of a bookstore or library that invites exploration.

One bookseller, a former schoolteacher, built up a successful business by helping readers find their personal constellations. The service he provided was marvelous, and based on an impossible method. Studying catalogs from the perspective of each of his customers, he would decide which books would interest which readers, and his predictions were almost always on target. He would buy book X for reader Z, and when Z appeared and browsed the new releases, he would make a happy discovery: a book that interested him. Naturally, if the encounter failed to occur, the book would remain on the shelf. In other words, the method involved anticipating the desires of a group of readers and risking the cost of failure.

We readers (not to mention writers) are annoyed when we can't find the books we want, right here and right now. It seems hard to understand why this should happen, considering the implicit model of an exhaustive distribution system that makes all books reach all corners of our universe. But books are sold or lent at more than a million points worldwide. Keeping a copy at each would surpass the demand for any title. And, reciprocally, there is no corner of the universe (not even the Library of Congress) where all books may be found. Their distribution is always incomplete and unpredictable. To write, publish, or distribute a book is like putting a message in a bottle and tossing it into the sea: its destination is uncertain. Yet time and again the miracle occurs: a book finds its reader, a reader finds his book.

To discover that an interesting book is out there waiting for us is a miracle, one we can't demand but can take advantage of by buying the book on the spot. Guesswork and luck play decisive roles in the encounter. We're unwilling to believe how improbable it is that we'll find the book we're looking for in a bookstore—whether we're looking because we know it exists, without knowing whether it exists, or even without knowing that we are looking at all until we find it.

In 1936, Margaret Mitchell's *Gone with the Wind* became the first novel to sell a million copies in a single year. Alexandra Ripley wrote a sequel, *Scar-*

lett, which sold 2.2 million copies in the last hundred days of 1991, thereby becoming "the fastest-selling novel in history, as well as, in retrospect, one of the most quickly forgotten" (Michael Korda, *Making the List: A Cultural History of the American Bestseller 1900–1999*). This historic maximum works out to 22,000 copies sold daily and 154,000 sold each week. But according to John Tebbel (*Between Covers: The Rise and Transformation of American Publishing*), by that point there were "more than 100,000 outlets ranging from bookstores to supermarkets and newsstands." Consequently (deducting book club, mail order, and export sales), the sales per outlet in those hundred extraordinary days reached a historic maximum of approximately one copy per week.

A book like *Scarlett* is available everywhere. But it isn't practical to sell most books in supermarkets, newsstands, or even many bookstores. To print one hundred thousand copies so that every outlet has a copy would be absurd for the majority of titles: a large part of the printing would be returned and remaindered. Most books sell only at selected outlets and never reach that top average sale of one copy per outlet per week. How to make sure they are in the right place at the right moment without a soothsayer? This is the question. Incorrect answers lead to costly consequences for the publisher, the bookseller, the reader, and the author. Put one copy here, none there; decide whether to reorder when the one copy sells, whether to return the unsold copy. Multiply these decisions for thousands of titles and thousands of outlets, and you end up with the usual mess: Here the book finds no reader; there the reader doesn't find the book. At each outlet, demand is minimal and thoroughly unpredictable. This is a typical stochastic model, an elegant name for chaos.

A good general bookstore carrying thirty thousand titles doesn't stock even 1 percent of all books available. Supposing the demand were the same for every title, the probability of the store not having a certain one would be 99 percent. If, under these circumstances, a stranger arrived blindfolded to take charge of the store and responded "We don't have it" to any request, 99 percent of the time he would be right. In practice, service fails in a smaller percentage of cases, because demand is not so broad (it isn't the same for every book, and is concentrated on certain titles); because the bookseller anticipates it with a degree of success and also shapes it by giving his store a certain identity; and finally, because readers adjust their expectations to the kind of store in which they shop. The adjustment is reciprocal: the bookseller imagines the constellations of books that will perfectly suit his readers and creates a type of store that attracts customers with matching expectations.

In a good bookstore, supply and demand are fortuitous, but not chaotic: they have a physiognomy, a recognizable identity, like constellations. The probability of finding a particular book increases in relation to the clarity of the store's focus, the diligence and shrewdness of the bookseller, and the size of the business. A few thousand titles may be very attractive to the reader, if they include everything that interests him. Totalities do exist on a small scale. They are like lists of recommended books, or complete bibliographies on particular subjects. Prestigious publishing houses are another example. Their catalogues are attractive, although they feature only dozens or hundreds of books, a ridiculous number when compared to the selection of any bookstore. The important thing is the way the whole is shaped with regard to a certain subject, criterion, locale, or clientele. A small, well-ordered collection can be practically exhaustive for certain constellations and may produce more fortunate encounters than a much larger but more amorphous collection. By the same token, a specialty bookstore with three thousand titles in stock needs a clearer focus and sharper aim than a general bookstore that stocks thirty thousand titles. The sharpest aim of all is required when the whole is defined (as in the case of the bookseller-mentor) not in relation to a single subject, but to a community of readers. In contrast, at an encyclopedic bookseller like Amazon.com, the probabilities are increased by the breadth of the selection — but not on just any scale. Once Amazon exists, an encyclopedic bookstore that is one tenth as large becomes much less attractive as a general resource, though it may preserve its appeal as a specialized resource (medical, for example). Nevertheless, barring exceptions like Amazon (with its millions of titles), the constellation factor carries more weight than the factor of scale.

Perfect service may be achieved in one of two ways: by stocking every book in the world or by employing a soothsayer. The advantage of the soothsayer is the ridiculous opposite extreme: the bookseller would need to keep on hand only the number of books that were going to be requested that day. The customer would discover that everything he was going to buy (or would have the impulse to buy) was there waiting for him, and there would never be a single extra book on the shelves. Since these solutions are impossible, in practice the bookseller tries in part to have everything (or at least everything fitting a certain profile) and in part to guess, with terrible results for seller and reader alike: no one asks for the available books, and the books they ask for are never in stock.

Each reader is a world: no two personal libraries are identical. The number of books is practically infinite, but the resources of the bookseller are finite. It is very likely that resources will be devoted to an assortment of books that no one wants. This is why selling books is a difficult business. If the bookseller buys a book that is sold quickly, and with those funds buys another book that sells quickly, and so on, he enters a virtuous cycle of expansion and service: he makes money, improves his selection, increases the number of happy encounters. But if he buys a book that doesn't sell, even if he has the right to return it to the publishing house, the cycle is vicious: he doesn't sell the book in question or any of the others he might have sold in successive cycles.

If the bookseller can return the book, he loses the shipping and packing costs, as well as the time and space he devoted to offering a title that no one wanted. His service capacity has failed the reader, the author, and the publishing house, with negative consequences for all involved. If he can't return the book, his situation is worse. The budget available for new purchases shrinks; the selection becomes dated and generates progressively less traffic (customers see fewer new titles each time they come in, and stop coming); less is sold, but costs are not reduced; the diminished stock that really moves and generates income must carry the dead stock and is finally crushed by the burden; income becomes insufficient to renew inventory, pay costs, and cover debts.

What is most notable about these failures is that they can occur when bookshelves are loaded with good books. But what is a good book when no one knows where it is or requests it? Outside of the place and moment in which it participates in a fortunate encounter with a reader, a book is not worth the paper it's printed on: it is trash littering the street, or floating on the sea. Its usefulness is reduced to its recyclable cellulose content. The best books can become trash if they are randomly placed in the wrong bookstores, libraries, or catalogs; if they are shelved out of order; if they are hidden away in a place that is difficult to reach; if there are physical, scheduling, or transaction obstacles to their purchase; or if the reader is told they are not available when they are. They can also become trash simply by being part of neglected collections: no one visits a bookstore or a library that lacks selection or sense. A book outside the constellation in which it makes sense is an orphaned book.

There are so many books, and almost all of them are worth less than the effort of searching for them unsuccessfully in many places, or the expense of making them reach every single one of their potential readers. A fortunate encounter can be priceless, but how much time is anyone able to devote to the buying or selling of a book? A single book is so cheap that it can't absorb much of the expense of publicity or searches; of making it arrive or having it sent; of packaging, storing, shipping, opening an account, billing, charging, taking returns, informing readers, informing oneself. The costs can be disproportionate for such a small transaction.

A book lost in the chaos is hopelessly lost. Who will undertake a costly expedition to find and rescue it? The fundamental demand to be made of any bookstore is that its collection take a shape that is informative in and of itself; it must have a distinct identity, so that readers can tell easily what fits and what doesn't. A distinct identity attracts attention, and orients the person who is searching. This is the secret of the magnetic appeal of certain assemblages: noise becomes music; scattered stars acquire an outline, names, and even legends, and become recognizable constellations that guide navigation. Good assemblages rescue books lost in the chaos, and produce the greatest number of fortunate encounters at the smallest possible cost, lots of reader traffic, and plenty of turnover per unit of investment, fixed costs, and reader effort expended.

A book correctly placed heightens the attraction of an entire collection, and when the whole takes on a coherent shape, the book is found more easily by its intended readers. In the same way, the articles in a good magazine reinforce one another and make the magazine attractive, like an interesting constellation, enlivening the exchange of a gathering of authors and readers. If what a magazine (or bookstore or library or publishing house) has to offer is chaotic, the cost for readers is high and discouraging, even if, hoping to find a miracle buried in the trash, they are able do the job the publisher (or bookseller or librarian) neglected to do. Just like writers, who make things out of words that are not theirs, inventive publishers, booksellers, librarians, teachers, anthologizers, and critics gather texts that are not theirs into meaningful and appealing assemblages.

It bothers us when we can't find a book, the very book that should be where we want it to be at the precise instant we want it. We accuse booksellers of being incompetent, if not of conspiring against the one marvelous book that by rights should be everywhere in the universe. In a bookstore I visited often and came to know by heart, I was once absurdly pleased to be able to direct a customer to a book that he had just been told the store "didn't have." Then, upon observing booksellers, befriending some of them, and reflecting on their difficulties, I realized that their task is impossible. Though there may be—and are—both excellent and incompetent booksellers, the underlying problem goes beyond individual ability. To be angry because a book isn't where you want it to be is to be angry at the randomness of fate.

Instead, we must take joy in fate, embrace it, celebrate it, explore bookstores in hope of a miracle. As Heraclitus said, if you don't expect the unexpected, you won't find it. In our wanderings across islands of overloaded shelves, on deserted beaches, and even in those floating garbage dumps that bob alongside piers, a fortunate encounter may come swimming along: the message in the bottle you've been waiting for.

In Search of the Reader

IN HIS *Confessions*, Saint Augustine tells of receiving a message sung from heaven: "Take this and read it." His life was changed by the discovery of a letter from Saint Paul seemingly written just for him. But how shall we marshal the angels so that they provide the same service for all of us? There are "infinite" books in the world, and "infinite" people. Who will match these two infinites to yield the short list of encounters ordained by the content of a text and a reader's personal history?

In most cases, a book's natural audience is limited to the hundreds or thousands of people to whom it has something to say. They are so few that a list of them might be practical. But no one knows how to find their names, print the correct number of copies of the book, distribute those copies around the planet, and alert the proper readers. *This book was written for you: here it is, now read it.* Human intermediaries (publishers, distributors, booksellers, librarians, critics, teachers, parents, friends) do what they can. The history of the book is full of efforts to facilitate these encounters.

The primordial effort was prehistoric. It consisted of committing to memory a few eloquent words, which had been spoken and seemed worthy of repetition so that others might hear them. In this way, we passed from ephemeral speech to the creation of a memorable text: from sentences to songs, stories, speeches, and finally, monumental works like the Homeric poems, which were memorized and passed on orally. This system for the reproduction and distribution of texts has not disappeared. It is still the means of circulation for many sentences, most jokes, a fair bit of social criticism, urban legends, the anecdotes and aphorisms of contemporary tribes, and of course, traditional oral literature. Telephone, radio, and television have all strengthened this prehistoric system.

Writing appeared next: the physical commitment of words to stone, pottery, papyrus, parchment, wax, paper, and photographic, phonographic, and electronic recordings. These new systems coexist with the original system. In some ways they reinforce it (transcriptions and recordings can extend the reach of oral communications, and when memory fails, refresh or correct them); in some ways they modify it (if transcriptions or recordings exist, improvisation is less free, a standard version is established, and there are fewer local variants); but above all, they multiply our opportunities for creating, reproducing, and distributing memorable texts in new ways.

The preservation of texts and other works in a physical medium is an external support of biological memory that facilitates creation. A story can be composed and told from memory, but not a novel. A song can be composed and sung from memory. But how to paint and exhibit a painting from memory? The physical preservation of creative work didn't only extend collective memory in time and space. It also made it possible for the human species to build a creative heritage, thus accelerating human development. In particular, it permitted the emergence of the individual reader, the individual author, the individual publisher, the individual critic. In oral literature, these roles only exist in embryo; barely assumed or recognized, they are lost in anonymity or attribution to legendary sources. But preservation also permitted new forms of anonymity: the pamphlets of the eighteenth century, the samizdat of the twentieth century, the jokes, criticism, and clandestine distribution of texts that circulate on the Web.

Some physical systems have disappeared: writing on wax tablets (revived by Edison with his phonographic cylinders only to vanish again); recordings on 78-rpm records. There is never any shortage of Cassandras proclaiming the end of other systems. But just as plastic and aluminum haven't eliminated the use of copper and iron, writing on paper and the printing of books may last for a very long time. Like copper and iron, they will perhaps be transformed and settle into new competitive niches. In fact, rather than diminishing, demand for paper has increased with the advent of electronic systems. It is these systems themselves that have so far had very short lives. Given the rapid changes in hardware and software, digital texts from just a few years ago may be harder to preserve and read than books printed centuries ago, or thousand-year-old manuscripts.

Reproduction and distribution with stock. The printing press with movable type was the precursor of modern industry: a system of interchangeable parts (characters) that permitted the making of very different products (books) in a repetitive fashion, more cheaply than the artisanal production of individual volumes (copied by hand). At the same time, there arose a fundamental problem common to all modern manufactured products: inventory.

When books were reproduced by copyists, who transcribed them one by one, the problem didn't exist. Each copy was, in effect, produced on demand. The printing press created the need to amass stock, the problem of financing it, and the risk that it might prove impossible to sell. For books with guaranteed sales, like the Bible, capitalists financed production, entered the distribution business, and finally became publishers themselves. For other books, the risk was reduced through selling by subscription. The subscription system has not disappeared, although ever since publishers began to assume the business risk of producing at their own expense and financing the whole process themselves, it has become less important.

This risk is fundamental. Almost all of a publisher's capital is tied up in advances to authors, inventory (paper, books in process, books in the warehouse, and books sold with the right to return), and credit extended to distributors and booksellers. By the time the investment in a first printing of a book is recouped, months or years have passed since the initial outlay. More often than not, the cycle ends with the warehousing of books that can't be sold, which must then either be remaindered or destroyed, and which diminish the capital available for the publication of other books.

Stocks of unsold copies don't exist in the case of periodicals, because almost no one is interested in yesterday's newspaper. Returns are destroyed, and the waste is paid for by advertisers and readers as part of the standard cost of the product. Something of this way of thinking has been passing from the press to the world of books, perhaps ever since mass market paperbacks began to circulate along newspaper distribution channels. Books began to be thought of as magazines, with a short shelf life, which reduced the chances of book and reader finding each other. But the interest of readers is not so fleeting. This reality, combined with publishers' hopes and a general horror at the destruction of books, encourages the keeping of too many books in stock. The cost is not as visible as it is for newspapers and, as a result, is paid by the publisher rather than the reader.

Stanley Unwin, in *The Truth About Publishing*, emphasized the hidden losses in stock: "Nearly all publishers deceive themselves—often quite unconsciously—and over-value their stock. Many publishers would be unable to look their profit and loss account in the face if they dealt really adequately with depreciation. . . . A great many publishers would be thankful to turn their entire stock into cash at the figure at which it appears in their balance sheet, and when that is so, it is quite certainly over-valued."

Some seemingly conservative accounting traditions help publishers fool themselves. The cost of each book is calculated by dividing by the number of copies produced, not the number of copies that will actually be sold, for the obvious reason that the first number is known and the second is not. Also, stock is valued at its cost, not at the price of sale, which is conservative for copies that actually will sell, but not for those that won't.

Another error is made when publishers set the price of sale according to the unit cost and ignore the risk of stock. To do this is actually to adopt the perspective of the printer. As far as the printer is concerned, every copy is sold from the outset (to the publisher). The problem of stock is not their problem. When more copies are printed, sales rise, costs are reduced, and profits increase, although part of this benefit is passed on to the publisher in the form of a cheaper unit cost. In contrast, the problem for the publisher, for whom sales are not guaranteed, is buying too much: there is a loss hidden in his stock that will sooner or later become visible.

If every thousand dollars of expense incurred up to the minute a book is printed (translating, editing, design, typesetting, negatives, press preparation) is divided by one thousand printed copies, then two thousand, then three thousand, and so forth, it may be supposed that unit costs are "decreasing" from $1.00 to $0.50, $0.33, $0.25, $0.20, etc., per copy. But there is something deceptive about these calculations. No matter the number of copies, the thousand dollars is already sunk and always the same, never less. What actually changes is that the second thousand copies are less likely to sell than the first thousand, the third thousand even less likely, and so on. Each additional thousand is more likely to be a mistake.

Unwin: "Frequently a book is worth publishing if it can be issued at no more than a certain figure, but liable to failure if published at a higher price. . . . Many a good book cannot be published except at a loss solely because of price limitations. . . . It must be borne in mind that the cost of typesetting remains the same whatever the number printed. . . . With this in mind the production manager may point out that if double the number were printed, or even an extra thousand, there would be no difficulty about publishing at the desired [price. . . . The] published price would have to be at least five times the manufacturing cost. In the USA it is at least six times. . . . But to let the desire to publish at a given price determine the number to be printed, instead of probable demand, is both a snare and a delusion."

The cost of making a mistake is not a concept itemized in accounting statements, but it is a basic reality in the book world. The author who works for years on a failed book; the publisher of a book that must finally be remaindered; the bookstore that is unable to sell the book; the disappointed reader who doesn't finish reading the book (or even worse, does): all made a mistake and paid the price. Paradoxically, the unsold stock held by publishers and booksellers is recorded as an asset on financial balance sheets. Trees turned to waste are recorded as economic growth. Mediocre, unnecessary, and frankly bad books are counted as academic credits, swelling the scholarly capital of authors and institutions.

With an army of angels at their command, publishers could know the exact demand in advance, its evolution over time, and its distribution by city. They would have a list of the readers interested in a particular title, with addresses and telephone numbers so they could alert them and sell them the book, which would be printed and reprinted in exactly the right quantities. This would eliminate returns and the waste of stock. (It would also lead to direct sales in many cases.) But human intermediaries aren't angels. Editorial experience amply demonstrates how easy it is to make a mistake in judging a book, on literary merits as well as sales potential.

In 1911, André Gide turned down *Du Côté de chez Swann,* by Marcel Proust. In 1964, a McGraw-

Hill editor rejected *The Peter Principle* by Lawrence J. Peter, with the following words: "I can foresee no commercial possibilities for such a book" (André Bernard, *Rotten Rejections*). Costly errors are also made in the opposite direction (advances, publicity costs, and excessively large printings), as recorded in the pages of *Publishers Weekly*. But the most frequent errors make no noise. They accumulate silently, in stock.

Reproduction and distribution without stock. For industry in general, the Japanese invented "just in time" systems of synchronization (which reduce inventory to a minimum) and systems of production en route (manufacturing takes place in the hold of a ship on its way to market, thereby integrating and reducing stocks of goods in process, goods in transit, and finished goods). The utopian ideal of contemporary industry is to return, in a certain sense, to artisanal production: to take the order of each customer individually, eliminating stores, distributors, and stock of finished products. The most notable example of this so far is the success of Dell, which assembles its computers according to individual specifications (from a very exten-

sive list of options) and sends them directly to customers' homes. The future of the book partakes of
this utopian ideal and embraces others of its own,
in particular the dream of the ultimate library.

The ancients saw the universe as a book and
dreamed of recreating it in the mirror of a library.
In 1941, Borges took this fantasy to its extreme:
"The Library of Babel" would include even those
books still to be written. Some years later, Van-
nevar Bush proposed what today we call hyper-
text: the electronic linking of all texts. "A library
of a million volumes could be compressed into one
end of a desk. [All of the printed material] the
human race has produced since the invention of
movable type . . . could be lugged off in a moving
van." A mechanism called Memex (memory extension) would automatically work just like memory,
connecting what mattered, and forgetting everything else. "One cannot hope thus to equal the
speed and flexibility with which the mind follows
an associative trail, but it should be possible to
beat the mind decisively in regard to the perma-
nence and clarity of the items resurrected from
storage. . . . Thus science may implement the ways
in which man produces, stores, and consults the

record of the race" ("As We May Think," *The At-lantic Monthly*, July 1945).

The medieval Bible was an early form of this project: a mirror of the universe in which all sacred books were gathered and connected hypertextually with references, concordances, and commentaries. To achieve something similar on the Web — a digital universal library including the full text of all books, from all eras, in every language — would be difficult and costly but technically possible.

In its radical form, this fantasy eliminates not only all inventory but also all intermediaries. In theory, accessing a text on screen should be easier, cheaper, and more appealing than turning to the bound book, with no need for warehouses, bookstores, or libraries. In theory, intermediaries would not be needed: the writer could appeal directly to the reader, as many writers who put their texts up free on the Web already do, and as Stephen King tried to do on a large commercial scale. But God is in the practical details, which seem to suggest that digital technology is destined to supplement rather than replace the printed book and its purveyors.

Digital systems of printing on demand eliminate the need to keep inventory on hand. Instead of producing a thousand copies or more of every signature, and folding, collating, and binding a thousand copies of a book — as traditional presses and binderies do; and instead of photocopying a single page a thousand times, then the next page, and so on, in order to assemble a thousand copies — as a simple copier would do; the new machines, like the old copyists, can photocopy or electronically print a single complete copy, from first page to last. This way, the printer can no longer say to the publisher, "I'll charge you less per copy if you print more." By the very nature of the process, he has to charge the same amount, even if the order is small.

The great rotary presses for the mass production of paperbacks also function without generating goods in process, but using them to produce a few thousand copies is not cost-effective. Nor is it cost-effective to use traditional presses to produce a few hundred copies. Print-on-demand systems can easily produce dozens of copies, or even a single copy. They are competitive for the smallest print runs, for books of standard quality. Their most important function will be to increase the lifespan of titles that are not now cost-effective to reprint.

Reprinting in small quantities allows a publisher's whole backlist to remain in print, although the demand for some titles may fall to one hundred or even ten copies a year. (The most extreme case, according to the *Guinness Book of World Records,* was that of a translation from Coptic to Latin that Oxford University Press sold at a rate of 2.6 copies a year from 1716 to 1907.) The traditional solution (reprinting at least a thousand copies) means that many titles go out of print, even if they were once bestsellers or fit neatly into the backlist. But when very small quantities can be reprinted, the publisher's investment and risk become manageable. This possibility may be taken into account from the moment the first printing is ordered.

If a publisher is convinced he can sell two thousand copies of a book, but not sure he can sell three, he can print two thousand in the traditional fashion and wait to see what happens, with the assurance that he will be able to print more if necessary, according to demand. If he sells three hundred more, which cost him six dollars per copy, he will have made a completely safe investment of eighteen hundred dollars in small payments over a period of time, which is very different from risking three thousand dollars in a single payment in advance to print a thousand extra copies up front and store them in case they are needed. Even if the unit cost of print-on-demand is twice as much (an illusory comparison because books printed by traditional methods cannot be ordered one at a time but only by the thousands), the difference is amply justified as insurance against the hidden loss of keeping seven hundred unsellable copies in the warehouse, which raises the real cost of the three hundred sold to ten dollars each, plus interest and storage. It is only logical that the translation from Coptic to Latin should be printed copy by copy from its very first printing.

The new machines can be located at various points on the circuit: with the printer, the publisher, the distributor, or a specialized print-on-demand service. The business implications vary depending on their placement. If it became practical for every bookstore to own a machine, returns would be a thing of the past. If machines became as compact and cheap as desktop printers, they could be kept in readers' homes. This would mean the realization of the universal digital library, with any reader able to download any book from the Internet to his screen or printer, just as it is now possible to download (in loose pages) thousands of classics digitalized by Project Gutenberg Association volunteers.

It is not surprising that so many people prefer to pay for traditional editions when they may read books for free on screen or printed on loose pages (at a printing cost per page that isn't always less than the cost per page of a traditional book). Looking up something onscreen or printing out a few pages is not the same as reading the entire text from the screen or printing it on your own printer. The content may be identical, but the visual, tactile, and even olfactory experience can make a lot of difference to the reader. Even if the hypertextual capacity of the electronic version is, in principle, superior to that of traditional indexes (which not all books have), there are many practical ways in which the traditional book is superior. On the most basic level, there is no need to have a machine running in front of you, with the text up on the screen. This practical advantage, and many others (portability, the lesser likelihood of theft, the impossibility of lending a book to a friend without the proper reading device, author's rights), tend to be ignored in futuristic fantasies, but they influence the decisions readers make. The lack of enthusiasm for e-books can't be attributed to the technophobia of common readers, because it also occurs, according to two surveys, among "advanced users of technology" and students reading textbooks (*Publishers Weekly*, September 9, 2002).

The practical details are critical, and they have unexpected ramifications, sometimes making devices suitable for unintended uses. The e-book wasn't invented for the visually impaired, but it turned out to be ideal for large-print reading. In the same way, when McGraw-Hill launched electronic versions of its scientific books, it thought that readers would most appreciate them for their content and hypertextuality and for the advantage of getting the text three months before it appeared in its print version (which would eventually be phased out). Surprisingly, although there were sales of e-books, the demand for the printed books rose. The advertising for the electronic version made more readers aware of the text, and they became interested in buying the print version after reading sample pages onscreen. Building on that experience, and on the software industry tradition of issuing pre-releases or beta versions (in order to introduce programs, invite users to test them, and gather opinions), McGraw-Hill created the site Betabooks, which allows readers to sample and order books that have not yet been published.

Seth Godin, author of the bestseller *Permission Marketing*, had a similar experience. After giving away 125,000 copies of *Unleashing the Ideavirus* on www.ideavirus.com, he received enough orders to print 28,000 copies (*Publishers Weekly*, September 18, 2000). The book, still available as a free download (permission is given to print, but not to bind), continues to sell as a hardcover, paperback, and e-book. Godin compares free Web distribution with the free distribution of music on the radio: "For a while, the music business fought the idea of radio stations playing songs for little or no compensation. Then, in the 1950s, they realized how valuable airplay was—so valuable that a congressional inquiry discovered that music labels were bribing disc jockeys to play their records." Another example might be given: public libraries.

In practice, they are a mainstay of the book market, though theoretically it might be thought that no one would buy a book he could read for free.

Amazon, which caused a revolution in every retail market when it began to sell books online in 1995, expanded its offerings to include e-books and used books at the same time it started to sell music and many other products. Considering the common technological inclination of online buyers, online sellers, and the publishers of e-books, it might have seemed logical for e-books to be the biggest success. Nevertheless, the true boom came with the sale of used books. According to the second quarterly report of 2002, third party transactions (primarily of used books) represented 35 percent of orders and 20 percent of units sold. This suggests that most of the orders for used books are for single copies, ordered from the thousands of booksellers who sell through Amazon and supply readers directly. It also suggests that digital technology, as in the case of print-on-demand, allows sellers to take better advantage of their stock, lengthens the lifecycle of titles, and increases the reader's diversity of choice.

Digital technology, admirably exploited by Amazon, attracts so much attention that it distracts from the company's traditional values, without which Amazon could not have succeeded: strong service, credibility, the quick incorporation of new titles, ample selection, and permanent availability of stock. All of these virtues have long been possessed by other good booksellers, and many are now taking advantage of digital technologies in individual or collective projects like the American Booksellers Association's Booksense.com. Independent bookstores, especially, which had lost market share to the big chains, don't seem to be on their way to extinction as a result of Amazon's rise. According to a survey by Ipsos Book Trends (*Publishers Weekly*, September 9, 2002), in the first half of the year 2002, readers bought 557 million adult trade books (up 1.6 percent over the same period in 2001). The market share in units decreased for the chains (from 22.2 to 21.4 percent), bookclubs (22.1 to 19.6 percent), and mail-order sales (3.3 to 2.8 percent), but it rose for independent booksellers (13.5 to 14.4 percent), online sales (7.4 to 8.4 percent) and used books (3.1 to 5.0 percent).

Reproduction and distribution without inter-mediaries. Two friends don't need the help of in-termediaries to talk to each other by phone. Many Renaissance and Baroque poems were copied by hand and circulated among the authors' friends, although the printing press already existed. Today, photocopiers, fax machines, and electronic mail allow friends to reproduce and distribute unpub-lished texts among themselves. Editors, publish-ers, distributors, booksellers, critics, teachers, par-ents, and friends are needed only when a polished text must be delivered to anonymous readers — our unknown friends.

The text itself is an invitation to the anonymous reader. Ideally, it would suffice to leave it lying in a park or to post it on the Web in order for its nat-ural audience to find it. The invisible hand of fate sometimes rescues a text lost in the chaos. But the intervention of angels or human intermediaries makes the extraordinary difference between con-versation and chaos. Intermediaries filter the chaos and create meaningful constellations, facili-tating the writer's exchange with the reader.

Even the utopia of a universal virtual library that includes every book in the world requires intermediaries to choose the books (not every stringing-together of words qualifies); select the proper versions (the study of textual variants, begun at the library of Alexandria with Homer, today takes on Joyce with the aid of computers, but will never be purely mechanical); edit them (books must be presented in legible form, and not just typographically); catalogue, distribute, critique, and recommend them. Naturally, all this mediation could happen on the Web, which might make sense if the text in question were a translation from Coptic to Latin. And naturally, the writer could be his own intermediary, as so many have been and will continue to be. But it isn't easy for prospective readers, those still-unknown friends, to discover without any outside assistance one writer among millions.

Independent of technological and economic circumstances, intermediaries will continue to make the difference between daunting chaos and a diversity that encourages dialogue. Culture is conversation, and the role of the intermediary is to shape that conversation and give new meaning to readers' lives simply by helping them find the books they need to read.

Diversity and Concentration

AS TEXTS, BOOKS ARE PART of a conversation that tends toward diversity. As commercial objects, they are part of the world of business, in which ideas and realities favor economic concentration. It is possible for these two qualities to reinforce each other, as Amazon's success proves (concentration bolstered by diversity), but other forms of concentration (conglomerates, bestsellers) have not promoted diversity, although they haven't been able to eliminate it, either.

At the beginning of the twentieth century, there were thousands of automobile makers (in fact, shops building units to order), thousands of homebuilders, and thousands of book publishers. A century later, the automobile makers have disappeared—only a few industrial manufacturing giants remain. But neither homebuilders nor publishers have suffered the same fate, despite the existence of big conglomerates. Diverse and dispersed production continues to be competitive. This has to do with the nature of books and houses. Not everything lends itself to industrial concentration.

The book business has pioneered practices that have spread to other fields, like the printing press with movable type, and online retailing. In its turn, it has adopted practices initiated in other industries. Bookstores weren't the first to allow their customers direct access to merchandise (permitting them to handle items without the sort of intervention by a clerk that is required in jewelry stores). But this practice made particular sense for books, and has been developed to the point where stores provide armchairs for reading. Other changes have been less fortunate.

A famous *Harvard Business Review* article by Theodore Levitt ("Marketing Myopia," *Harvard Business Review,* July–August 1960, of which more than one hundred thousand reprints were sold) criticized the failure of railroad companies at the beginning of the twentieth century to seize the opportunity of highway transportation as a means of furthering their growth (by offering service linking railroads and highways, for example) "because they assumed themselves to be in the railroad business rather than in the transportation business." The article prompted a quest for wider horizons in many industries, which began to ask themselves: What kind of business are we really in? This may have been the intellectual origin of the conglomerates which today try to integrate books, newspapers, magazines, film, radio, music, television, and the Internet into a broader concept, namely, the media. In theory, the affinities are obvious. The intent in every case is to produce, reproduce, and distribute content. And in many cases, the content passing from one medium to another is the same (Harry Potter, for example). In theory, merging should give rise to economies of scale and combined operations (or synergy). Nevertheless, in practice and in terms of the bottom line, the hoped-for synergies have been disappointing.

The management practices which derive from the application of Pareto's Law—80 percent of profits come from 20 percent of products—have led to disappointing results. Disappointing, too, is the imperative that every undertaking return a profit. Concentrating on the most profitable and getting rid of all the rest in order to increase the company's profits may be effective, but it can also be destructive: eliminating future moneymakers, doing away with low-grossing resources that serve as necessary context for the functioning of big earners, and rendering the company's mission meaningless. Many publishers and booksellers who had businesses that made sense were bought out by conglomerates that didn't understand them, mutilated them, then didn't have the success they expected and abandoned them.

Good publishers and booksellers see books from both perspectives: as texts (around which conversations must be organized and attractive constellations created) and as commercial objects. This means that money will inevitably be lost on some titles, whether by mistake or out of necessity (when books with low sales occupy a natural place in the constellation). The trick is to insure that money isn't lost on most titles and that some are successful enough to make the whole operation profitable. When this double perspective is re-duced to a single perspective—the quarterly earnings reports — the constellation becomes less interesting, while the quarterly profits don't necessarily increase.

The greater part of the profits of a publishing house is made on just a few titles, and sometimes just one. The tradition was originally to take advantage of this reality. A good writer whose sales were small was kept on by a good publisher (thanks to the money brought in by better-selling writers) because his work had a place in the constellation and there was some hope that in the future it would generate, in its turn, money for the support of other good writers. Of course, since the nineteenth century, there have been authors (like Washington Irving and Mark Twain) who were conscious of the exceptional importance of one of their books in their publishers' accounts and who, refusing to bow to tradition, obtained special bonuses or printed and distributed their books themselves rather than subsidize their publishers and less fortunate colleagues.

But the literary agents and the conglomerates of the twentieth century created a market focused on bestsellers, which plucked financial stars from the constellations where they made sense and set them in another kind of "constellation"—the star system. At the same time, the financial horizon, the life-cycle of books, and the employment cycles of publishers in the service of conglomerates were shortened. Independent publishers, who weren't well-paid executives in constant rotation but owners content to earn little because they enjoyed their freedom and were able to think in terms of decades, lost their major source of funding for the longterm development of new authors to executives who thought in quarterly terms and had to engineer spectacular coups for the larger public, the mass media, and the banks.

The first stage was relatively easy, because it involved skimming writers from painstakingly formed constellations with irresistible offers. Then it became necessary to invent instant stars by investing big money and taking big risks. The reason it is possible to make amazing profits from huge sales is that the average price of books is set according to titles that sell just a few thousand copies. On that basis, a book that recovers its initial costs in hardcover and continues to sell has a high profit margin in paperback (even though the price is lower), multiplied by a greater volume of sales. The volume can be extraordinary for the bestsellers of the star system, but unlike trade paperbacks, they require onerous contracts, major bonuses, additional costs, and large investments (advances, promotion, big first printings) that may prove to be unrecoverable if fewer books sell than calculated. It is a serious, highly speculative gamble.

There are eloquent testaments by André Schiffrin in *The Business of Books* and Jason Epstein in *Book Business* to this evolution and its negative consequences, which express reasonable hopes for the future of diversity. It is impossible to believe that the book business will one day become like the automobile business, which squeezed small and medium-size producers out of the market. Books that require large capital investments by the publishers, such as blockbusters of the star system and big encyclopedias, are a segment of the market that lends itself well to concentration, but they aren't the whole market.

The book business can be profitable on almost any scale (in fact, medium-size operations may be riskier than small operations). The minimum investment required to participate is nothing like what is necessary for the production of automobiles and other industrial bestsellers. The development of a new pharmaceutical product requires years and hundreds of millions of dollars. But the development of Harry Potter (whose market is comparable to that of a pharmaceutical product) required no more than the personal sacrifice and talent of an unemployed person working from home. Personal sacrifice and talent have also made possible the creation of small publishing houses and bookstores that ultimately become profitable. The biggest editorial conglomerate in the world, Bertelsmann, began with the solitary efforts of a traveling Bible salesman. Editorial conglomerates and chain stores haven't driven all independent publishing houses, booksellers, and writers out of business. Will they do so in the future? It isn't likely. The development of pharmaceutical technologies have increased the minimum investment required to enter the market, but the new book business technologies have reduced it.

The historical trend toward a decrease in the relative cost of books persists. Books copied by hand on parchment were a luxury only the aristocracy could afford. Printing them on paper reduced the costs of labor and raw material. This made it possible to sell many more copies of the same titles, but not only that; it also made possible publication of many different titles. From the first books printed by Gutenberg to mass market paperbacks, prices have continued to drop. At the same time, the number of titles has exploded. The electronic reproduction and distribution of texts, with all its limitations, further lowers the cost of diversity, which continues to flourish.

In the second half of the twentieth century, college attendance grew extraordinarily. This increased the number of people who read, but more so that of people who write and want to be published. The idea of publishing as a form of personal realization has spread: "Eighty-one percent of Americans feel they should write a book, according to a survey of 1,006 adult Americans commissioned by the Jenkins Group, Inc. . . . Jenkins estimates that 6 million Americans have actually written a manuscript" (www.bookspublishing.com, Press Release, September 23, 2002). In the academic world, this personal aspiration becomes a professional requirement, summed up by the phrase "publish or perish." Academic books, professional books, and textbooks account for half of the market.

The diversity of subject matter is multiplied by the growth of knowledge, the proliferation of specialties, greater contact among countries and cultures, and social creativity on all levels. In a rich and educated society, the strangest of hobbies is able to interest a few thousand readers, which makes it worthwhile to publish a book on the subject. This increases the number of titles published per capita.

The technologies that lower the threshold for investment and the cost of the product respond to the need of a better-educated population to read and express itself in an ongoing conversation in which diverse subjects and interests multiply. By rooting themselves in this economic reality, some forms of concentration that actually favor diversity may thrive. But those that impoverish conversation instead of enriching it will encounter difficulties inherent in the very nature of books. There are many examples of acquisitions, mergers, and bestsellers that ultimately proved to be bad deals.

This concentration of profits around a few titles is an old reality but a dangerous model for planning. As publishers readily admit, they possess no sure formula for producing bestsellers. More important, readers don't buy only bestsellers. So the most attractive publishing constellations include many books with smaller sales. This situation presents opportunities for independent publishers and booksellers that are not available to conglomerates and chains. The trend to concentration in publishing has a limit, while the trend to diversity does not. Thus, the noise and emptiness of bestsellers poses less of a threat to reading than the noise and emptiness of chaos. Fortunately, there are still people and organizations willing to filter out the noise from the music, define constellations of books, and organize conversations for common consideration. So long as these traditions are alive, we may be confident that rich and nourishing diversity will prevail.